Explore
PYRENEES
Like A Local 2023

Your Ultimate Travel Companion to
Discover the Pyrenees' Best-Kept
Secrets and Thrilling Expeditions with
Insider Tips, A Locals Guide to
Authentic Experiences.

Alec James

Table of Contents

My Dad's First Visit to Pyrenees

I remember the day my dad returned from his first visit to the Pyrenees. The excitement in his voice was palpable as he narrated the story of his grand adventure to me. I sat on the edge of my seat, eager to hear every detail.

He began by describing the breathtaking landscapes that greeted him as he arrived in the Pyrenees. Towering snow-capped peaks, lush green valleys, and crystal-clear lakes stretched out before him, painting a picture of natural beauty that seemed almost surreal.

For his accommodation, my dad had chosen a cozy mountain chalet nestled in a small village. He spoke fondly of the warm hospitality of the locals and the rustic charm of his surroundings. From his window, he had a stunning view of the mountains that would be his playground for the next few days.

Outdoor activities were the highlight of his trip. He regaled me with tales of exhilarating hikes through verdant trails, where he felt like he was stepping into a postcard. He climbed to remote summits, basking in the glory of panoramic vistas that took his breath away. The air was crisp and invigorating, and he felt a sense of freedom and liberation with every step.

One of the most memorable experiences he had was rafting down the swift-flowing rivers of the Pyrenees. The adrenaline rush as he navigated the rapids, the laughter and camaraderie of his fellow rafters, and the refreshing splash of water on his face made for an unforgettable adventure.

Of course, my dad couldn't resist trying his hand at skiing. He laughed as he described his clumsy attempts to stay balanced on the slopes. But with the patient guidance of a local ski instructor, he gradually found his rhythm and soared down the powdery slopes, feeling an indescribable sense of joy and accomplishment.

But it wasn't just the outdoor activities that left an impression on him; the local cuisine was a gastronomic delight. He savoured hearty mountain stews, infused with rich flavours and local ingredients. He sampled artisanal cheeses and indulged in flaky pastries that melted in his mouth. Each meal was a celebration of Pyrenees' culinary heritage, leaving him eager to try more.

As he recounted his encounters with the locals, I could sense the warmth and genuine connection he had formed during his trip. He spoke of conversations shared over cups of steaming hot chocolate in cosy cafes, of impromptu chats with shepherds tending to their flocks in the mountains, and of the laughter and camaraderie he experienced at a lively village festival.

Listening to my dad's story, I could see the twinkle in his eyes and the passion in his voice. The Pyrenees had captured his heart, and I knew that he had left a piece of himself in those majestic mountains.

He concluded his tale with a smile, expressing his gratitude for the opportunity to experience such an incredible adventure. He urged me to visit the Pyrenees someday, to witness its beauty firsthand and create my own memories.

As I listened to his story, I couldn't help but be inspired. His passion for exploration and his eagerness to immerse himself in a new culture ignited a flame within me. The Pyrenees became more than just a distant destination; it became a symbol of the boundless possibilities that lay beyond our comfort zones.

From that day forward, the Pyrenees held a special place in my heart. And while I may not have been there physically, I felt like I had embarked on the journey with my dad, sharing in his adventures, his triumphs, and his awe-inspiring experiences. And someday, I knew that I too would stand amidst those majestic peaks, breathing in the same exhilarating air and creating my own story of the Pyrenees.

Date	Itinerary

CHAPTER ONE

Introduction to Pyrenees

The Pyrenees are a mountain range that forms a natural border between France and Spain. They are the second-highest mountain range in Europe, after the Alps, and stretch for over 430 miles (700 kilometres). The highest peak in the Pyrenees is Aneto, which is 11,168 feet (3,404 metres) tall. These magnificent mountains are renowned for their breathtaking landscapes, rich biodiversity, and vibrant cultural heritage.

The Pyrenees are a popular destination for outdoor enthusiasts, as they offer a variety of activities, including hiking, skiing, climbing, and biking. The region is also home to a number of charming villages and towns, as well as some of Europe's most beautiful scenery.

About the Pyrenees

The Pyrenees are a young mountain range, formed about 50 million years ago. They are the result of the collision of the Iberian and Eurasian plates. The mountains are still rising today, at a rate of about 1 millimetre per year.

The Pyrenees, often referred to as the "Mountain of the Basques," are a stunning geological formation. These mountains have a diverse range of peaks, valleys, rivers, and forests, offering an unparalleled experience for nature enthusiasts and adventure seekers alike.

One of the remarkable features of the Pyrenees is its impressive peaks. The range boasts an array of towering summits, including the renowned Pico de Aneto, which stands as the highest peak in the Pyrenees, reaching a staggering elevation of 3,404 metres. These majestic peaks attract mountaineers and hikers from around the world, providing them with challenging ascents and breathtaking panoramic views.

Beyond their physical grandeur, the Pyrenees are also home to an extraordinary ecosystem. The region is a sanctuary for diverse flora and fauna, with a remarkable blend of Mediterranean and alpine environments. The lower slopes of the mountains are adorned with lush forests of oak, beech, and pine trees, while the higher altitudes showcase alpine meadows and colourful wildflowers during the warmer months. This rich vegetation supports a wide range of animal species, including chamois, ibex, bears, wolves, and a plethora of bird species, making it a paradise for nature lovers and wildlife enthusiasts.

The Pyrenees are not only a haven for nature enthusiasts but also a treasure trove of cultural heritage. The region has a long and fascinating history, with traces of human presence dating back thousands of years. The Pyrenees have witnessed the rise and fall of ancient civilizations, including the Celts, Romans, and Visigoths, all of which have left their mark on the land. The villages nestled within the mountains reflect the traditional lifestyles and architectural charm of the region. Visitors can immerse themselves in the local culture, savour delicious regional cuisine, and participate in colourful festivals that celebrate the Pyrenean way of life.

For outdoor enthusiasts, the Pyrenees offer an extensive array of recreational activities throughout the year. During the summer months, hiking and mountaineering are popular pursuits, with an abundance of well-marked trails catering to different levels of experience. The Pyrenees are also renowned for their excellent opportunities for cycling, both on challenging mountain roads and picturesque valleys. As winter sets in, the mountains transform into a winter wonderland, attracting skiers and snowboarders to its numerous ski resorts, where they can carve their way down pristine slopes and enjoy the snowy landscapes.

The Pyrenees are an enchanting mountain range that captivates visitors with its awe-inspiring beauty, abundant wildlife, and rich cultural heritage. Whether you seek adventure, tranquillity, or an immersive cultural experience, the Pyrenees have something to offer for everyone. Exploring these majestic mountains will undoubtedly leave you with lifelong memories and a deep appreciation for the wonders of nature..

Culture and History

The Pyrenees region is not only blessed with stunning natural landscapes but also boasts a rich and vibrant cultural heritage. The Pyrenees region is a treasure trove of cultural richness and historical significance. From the diverse Pyrenean people and their unique languages to the distinctive architecture and captivating art forms, the Pyrenees offer a captivating glimpse into a vibrant and multifaceted cultural tapestry. Exploring the culture and history of the Pyrenees provides a deeper understanding and appreciation of this remarkable region and its enduring legacy.

The Pyrenean People

The Pyrenees have been inhabited by various civilizations throughout history, each leaving their mark on the region's cultural fabric. The people of the Pyrenees, known as Pyreneans, are warm, welcoming, and proud of their heritage. They have managed to preserve their traditional way of life while embracing modern influences.

The Pyrenean population consists of diverse ethnic groups, including Basques, Catalans, Aragonese, and Occitans. Each group has its distinct customs, traditions, and folklore, adding to the cultural tapestry of the region. These communities have a strong connection with the land and have developed unique practices, such as transhumance, the seasonal movement of livestock between different altitudes, which is still observed in some areas.

The Pyrenean Languages

One of the most intriguing aspects of the Pyrenees is its linguistic diversity. The region is home to several distinct languages, some of which are considered endangered. The Basque language, known as Euskara, is the most prominent non-Indo-European language in the Pyrenees and is spoken by the Basque people. It is a language isolate, meaning it has no known linguistic relatives.

In addition to Basque, other languages spoken in the Pyrenees include Catalan, Occitan, Aragonese, and Gascon.

Catalan is a Romance language that is closely related to Spanish and French. It is the official language of Andorra and the autonomous community of Catalonia in Spain. Catalan is also spoken in parts of France, Italy, and the Balearic Islands.

Basque is a non-Indo-European language that is not related to any other language in the world. It is the official language of the Basque Country in Spain and France. Basque is also spoken in parts of Navarre, La Rioja, and Aragon in Spain.

Occitan is a Romance language that is closely related to Catalan, Spanish, and French. It is the official language of the Occitanie region in France.

Occitan is also spoken in parts of Italy, Spain, and Andorra.

These languages have been influenced by neighbouring regions and have unique dialects specific to different areas of the Pyrenees. Language is an integral part of the Pyrenean cultural identity, and efforts are being made to preserve and revitalise these linguistic traditions.

Pyrenean Architecture

The Pyrenean region showcases a remarkable blend of architectural styles influenced by its historical and cultural context. Traditional Pyrenean architecture is characterised by sturdy stone structures with steep roofs, designed to withstand the harsh mountain climate. These buildings often feature wooden balconies and intricate carvings, reflecting the local craftsmanship.

One notable architectural feature in the Pyrenees is the "bordas." These are traditional mountain houses that were originally used for housing both humans and livestock. Bordas are typically constructed using local materials, such as stone and wood, and were built to adapt to the rugged terrain. Nowadays, some bordas have been converted into rural accommodations, allowing visitors to experience the charm of Pyrenean architecture firsthand.

Other notable architectural styles in Pyrenees include;

Romanesque architecture, which is characterised by its round arches and ribbed vaults. Romanesque architecture can be found in many churches and monasteries in the Pyrenees.

Gothic architecture, which is characterised by its pointed arches and ribbed vaults. Gothic architecture can be found in many cathedrals and churches in the Pyrenees.

Baroque architecture, which is characterised by its elaborate ornamentation and dramatic lighting. Baroque architecture can be found in many churches and palaces in the Pyrenees.

Traditional Pyrenean architecture, which is characterised by its use of stone, wood, and slate. Traditional Pyrenean architecture can be found in many villages and towns in the Pyrenees.

Pyrenean Art

Pyrenean art encompasses a wide range of expressions, including painting, sculpture, and crafts, reflecting the region's history, natural surroundings, and cultural traditions. Traditional Pyrenean art often draws inspiration from nature, with motifs such as flowers, animals, and landscapes being prevalent.

One notable form of Pyrenean art is "santons." These are small figurines carved out of wood or clay, depicting religious and folkloric characters. Santons are intricately crafted and are often used to recreate nativity scenes during Christmas celebrations. They represent the skilled craftsmanship and devotion to artistic expression in the Pyrenees.

In addition to visual art, music and dance are essential elements of Pyrenean culture. Traditional folk music, characterised by lively melodies and rhythmic beats, is performed at festivals and gatherings. Pyrenean dances, such as the "Sardana" in Catalonia and the "Fandango" in the Basque Country, are vibrant expressions of regional identity and community spirit.

The Pyrenees region is a treasure trove of cultural richness and historical significance. From the diverse Pyrenean people and their unique languages to the distinctive architecture and captivating art forms, the Pyrenees offer a captivating glimpse into a vibrant and multifaceted cultural tapestry. Exploring the culture and history of the Pyrenees provides a deeper understanding and appreciation of this remarkable region and its enduring legacy.

Why Visit the Pyrenees

There are numerous compelling reasons to visit the Pyrenees. Here are some key aspects that make the region an enticing destination:

1. Breathtaking Natural Beauty: The Pyrenees are renowned for their awe-inspiring landscapes. Majestic mountains, verdant valleys, crystal-clear lakes, and cascading waterfalls create a picturesque setting that is a paradise for nature lovers. Whether you enjoy hiking, skiing, or simply immersing yourself in the tranquillity of the great outdoors, the Pyrenees offer an abundance of breathtaking natural beauty to explore and enjoy.

2. Outdoor Activities: The Pyrenees provide an extensive range of outdoor activities for adventure enthusiasts. From exhilarating hikes and mountain biking to thrilling skiing and snowboarding in winter, the region offers endless opportunities to engage in exciting and challenging pursuits. With well-marked trails, world-class ski resorts, and diverse landscapes, the Pyrenees cater to both seasoned adventurers and those seeking more leisurely outdoor experiences.

3. Rich Cultural Heritage: The Pyrenees boast a fascinating cultural heritage shaped by centuries of history and diverse influences. The region is home to distinctive communities with their own customs, traditions, and languages. Visitors have the chance to explore charming villages, engage with friendly locals, and immerse themselves in the vibrant traditions and festivals that celebrate the Pyrenean way of life. Additionally, the Pyrenees are dotted with ancient castles, Romanesque churches, and historic sites that offer glimpses into the region's captivating past.

4. Culinary Delights: The Pyrenees are a gastronomic haven, offering a delightful fusion of flavours influenced by the region's rich culinary traditions. From hearty mountain cuisine featuring local specialties like hearty stews, cured meats, and artisan cheeses to the freshest seafood in coastal areas, the Pyrenees provide a diverse and delectable dining experience. Pair your meals with exceptional local wines, including those produced in the vineyards nestled at the foothills, to complete your culinary journey.

5. Wellness and Relaxation: The serene and pristine environment of the Pyrenees lends itself to rejuvenation and relaxation. The region is home to numerous thermal spas and wellness retreats where visitors can indulge in soothing treatments, hot spring baths, and wellness activities amidst a tranquil natural setting. Whether you seek solitude or a rejuvenating escape, the Pyrenees offer ample opportunities for wellness and relaxation.

6. Wildlife and Biodiversity: The Pyrenees boast a rich and diverse ecosystem, making it a paradise for wildlife enthusiasts and nature lovers. The mountains are home to a wide range of animal species, including chamois, ibex, eagles, and bears. Birdwatchers will be delighted by the variety of avian species that inhabit the region. Exploring the Pyrenees allows you to witness and appreciate the incredible biodiversity and conservation efforts in place to protect these natural habitats.

7. Scenic Drives and Panoramic Views: Driving through the Pyrenees is an experience in itself. The region offers stunning scenic routes and mountain passes that provide breathtaking views at every turn. Whether you embark on the famous Route des Cols or traverse the winding roads that snake through valleys and mountains, you'll be treated to panoramic vistas that will leave a lasting impression.

Visiting the Pyrenees allows you to immerse yourself in a world of natural beauty, adventure, rich cultural heritage, culinary delights, and relaxation. Whether you seek outdoor thrills, cultural exploration, or a serene retreat amidst breathtaking scenery, the Pyrenees offer an unforgettable experience that caters to a wide range of interests and preferences.

When to Visit

The best time to visit the Pyrenees depends on your interests and the activities you plan to engage in. Going through this guide will help you decide when it's more convenient for you to visit.

1. Spring (March to May): Spring brings mild temperatures and blooming landscapes to the Pyrenees. The mountains come alive with vibrant wildflowers, and the valleys are lush and green. This season is ideal for hiking, cycling, and exploring the region's natural beauty. However, it's worth noting that higher altitudes may still have snow during early spring, so be prepared accordingly.

2. Summer (June to August): Summer is a popular time to visit the Pyrenees, as the weather is generally warm and sunny. It's an excellent season for outdoor activities like hiking, mountain biking, and wildlife spotting. The mountain passes are open, and the ski resorts transform into adventure playgrounds with activities like zip-lining and rock climbing. The summer months also bring festivals, cultural events, and a vibrant atmosphere to the region.

3. Autumn (September to November): Autumn in the Pyrenees is a breathtaking season characterised by colourful foliage as the leaves change to hues of red, orange, and gold. The weather remains pleasant, making it an excellent time for hiking, photography, and enjoying the natural beauty of the region. Autumn is also the season for grape harvest and wine festivals, providing a chance to savour the local wines.

4. Winter (December to February): Winter in the Pyrenees is a wonderland for snow enthusiasts. The mountains are blanketed in snow, making it an ideal time for skiing, snowboarding, and other winter sports. The Pyrenees boast excellent ski resorts with a range of slopes catering to all skill levels. The cozy mountain villages offer a charming atmosphere, and thermal spas provide a warm retreat after a day in the snow.

It's important to note that weather conditions can vary in the Pyrenees, especially at higher elevations. Be prepared for temperature changes and check the local forecasts before your visit. Additionally, peak tourist season in the Pyrenees is during summer and winter, so if you prefer a quieter experience, consider visiting during spring or autumn when there are fewer crowds.

Ultimately, the best time to visit the Pyrenees depends on your preferences, whether you're seeking outdoor adventures, cultural events, or a tranquil retreat amidst nature's beauty.

Getting to the Pyrenees

There are many ways to get to the Pyrenees, depending on your starting point. Here are a few options:

1. By plane: There are several airports in the Pyrenees, including Toulouse-Blagnac Airport in France and Barcelona-El Prat Airport in Spain. From these airports, you can take a train, bus, or taxi to your destination in the Pyrenees.

2. By train: There are several train lines that run through the Pyrenees, including the TGV in France and the AVE in Spain. These trains can take you to major cities in the Pyrenees, such as Lourdes, Pau, and Barcelona.

3. By bus: There are also several bus lines that run through the Pyrenees. These buses can take you to smaller towns and villages in the Pyrenees.

4. By car: If you're driving to the Pyrenees, you can either take the main highways or one of the smaller, more scenic roads. The main highways are faster, but the smaller roads offer more stunning views.

Tips to Get Cheap Flights

- Be flexible with your travel dates because weekdays and off-season are frequently when you can find the lowest flights.

- Consider flying into a smaller airport. Airfares into smaller airports are frequently less expensive than those into larger ones.

- Use a search engine for flights. You may compare fares from several airlines using one of the numerous flight search tools that are available online.

- Subscribe to email updates. Numerous flight search engines include email alerts that will inform you when the cost of your selected flight changes.

- Consider a travel credit card. For free flights, some travel credit cards give points or miles that can be redeemed.

- Plan your travels in advance. Finding a decent deal is more likely the earlier you book your flights.

- Consider flying into another nearby country. If you're not set on travelling into France or Spain, you might be able to find cheaper flights into Andorra or Portugal.

- Seek out package deals. Package offers from some travel providers may include travel, lodging, and activities. These bundles are frequently an excellent way to save money.

- Check for student or senior discounts. Lots of airlines give discounts to students.

Make sure to book your flights or train tickets in advance, especially if you're travelling during peak season and if you're driving, be sure to check the weather conditions before you go.

CHAPTER TWO

Planning Your Trip

Planning a trip to the Pyrenees promises an unforgettable experience. This section will provide you with essential information to help you plan a successful and enjoyable journey to this stunning destination.

Visa and Entry Requirements

The Pyrenees are a mountain range that borders France and Spain therefore, you can enter the Pyrenees through both countries. The countries have different visa and entry requirements, so it is important to check with the embassy or consulate of the country you will be visiting to find out what is required.

Visa requirements for France

Citizens of most countries need a visa to visit France. The type of visa you will require depends on the intentions why you are visiting and the amount of time you want to stay. For example, if you are visiting France for tourism, you will need a short-stay visa. If you are visiting France for work or study, you will need a long-stay visa.

You can request for a visa at the French embassy or consulate in your home country. The application procedure can take several weeks, so it's necessary to apply in advance of your departure date.

Visa requirements for Spain

Citizens of most countries need a visa to visit Spain. The type of visa you will require depends on the intentions why you are visiting and the amount of time you want to stay. For example, if you are visiting Spain for tourism, you will need a short-stay visa. If you are visiting Spain for work or study, you will need a long-stay visa.

To acquire a visa you can go to the Spanish embassy or consulate in your home country. The application procedure can take several weeks, so it's necessary to apply in advance of your departure date.

Entry requirements

In addition to a visa, you will also need to meet certain entry requirements to enter the Pyrenees. These requirements include:

- A valid passport
- A return ticket
- Proof of accommodation
- Proof of financial means

You may also be asked to provide a medical certificate or a vaccination record.

Eligibility for visa

To be eligible for a visa to the Pyrenees, you must meet the following criteria:

- You must be a citizen of a country that requires a visa to visit France or Spain.
- You must have a valid passport.
- You must have a return ticket.
- You must have proof of accommodation.
- You must have proof of financial means.
- You may also be asked to provide a medical certificate or a vaccination record.

For more information on visa and entry requirements for the Pyrenees, you can contact the following embassies or consulates:

- French embassy in your home country
- Spanish embassy in your home country

You can also visit the websites of the French and Spanish governments for more information.

Currency and Money Matters

The currency and money matters of the Pyrenees are complex and have evolved over time. The region is home to two countries, Spain and France, and each country has its own currency. The euro is the official currency of Spain, while the euro and the French franc are both legal tender in France. In this guide, we will explore the various aspects of currency, banking, and financial transactions in the Pyrenees region, offering valuable insights for travellers and businesses alike.

In addition to the national currencies, there are also a number of regional currencies in use in the Pyrenees. The most well-known of these is the peseta, which was the official currency of Spain until 2002. The peseta is still widely used in the Pyrenees, particularly in rural areas.

Another regional currency that is used in the Pyrenees is the sou. The sou is a French coin that was first minted in the 13th century. The sou is no longer legal tender, but it is still used in some parts of the Pyrenees as a unit of account.

In addition to the national and regional currencies, there are also a number of foreign currencies that are used in the Pyrenees. The most common foreign currencies are the euro, the US dollar, and the British pound.

The use of different currencies in the Pyrenees can be confusing for tourists and locals alike. However, there are a number of resources available to help people understand the currency situation in the region. The websites of the Spanish and French central banks provide information on the national currencies.

Here are some additional information you should know about currency and money matters in the Pyrenees:

Currency

1. Euro: The Pyrenees region falls within the Eurozone, where the official currency is the Euro (€). The Euro is widely accepted throughout the Pyrenees, making it convenient for visitors from other Eurozone countries.

2. Currency Exchange: If you are travelling from a country with a different currency, you can exchange your money at banks, exchange offices, or ATMs available in major towns and cities. It is paramount to compare exchange rates and fees to get the best deal.

Banking and ATMs

1. Banks: Major towns in the Pyrenees have a range of banking services, including local and international banks. They offer services such as currency exchange, money transfers, and ATM facilities.

2. Automated Teller Machines (ATMs): ATMs are easily accessible in most towns and tourist areas. They provide a convenient way to withdraw cash, check balances, and conduct basic banking transactions. Ensure that your ATM card is compatible with international transactions.

Credit Cards and Payment Methods

1. Credit Cards: Credit cards, especially Visa and Mastercard, are widely accepted in hotels, restaurants, and shops in the Pyrenees. However, it's advisable to carry some cash for small establishments or places with limited card acceptance.

2. Contactless Payments: Contactless payment methods, such as mobile wallets and contactless cards, are gaining popularity in the Pyrenees. Many establishments have adapted to this technology, allowing for swift and secure transactions.

Tips for Handling Money

1. Cash vs. Card: It's advisable to carry a mix of cash and cards. Cash is handy for small purchases, local markets, and places where card acceptance might be limited. Cards provide convenience and security for larger transactions.

2. Currency Reservations: If you plan to visit remote areas or smaller towns, it's recommended to ensure you have enough cash in the local currency before your journey, as ATMs may not be readily available in such locations.

3. Safety and Security: Practise common-sense safety measures when handling money, such as keeping an eye on your belongings, using secure ATMs, and avoiding displaying large amounts of cash in public.

Understanding the currency and money matters in the Pyrenees region is essential for a smooth and hassle-free experience while travelling or conducting financial transactions. Whether you're exploring the stunning landscapes, indulging in local cuisine, or shopping for souvenirs, being informed about the currency, banking services, and payment methods will ensure that you can enjoy all that the Pyrenees has to offer with peace of mind.

Language and Communication

The Pyrenees are home to a diverse range of languages, reflecting the region's history and geography. The most widely spoken languages in the Pyrenees are Spanish and French, which are the official languages of Spain and France respectively.

In addition to Spanish and French, there are a number of regional languages spoken in the Pyrenees. These include:

● **Catalan:** Catalan is a Romance language that is spoken in the northeastern Pyrenees, in the regions of Catalonia, Aragon, and Valencia.

- **Occitan:** Occitan is another Romance language that is spoken in the southwestern Pyrenees, in the regions of Languedoc-Roussillon, Midi-Pyrénées, and Aquitaine.

- **Basque:** Basque is a non-Indo-European language that is spoken in the western Pyrenees, in the Basque Country.

There are also a number of minority languages spoken in the Pyrenees, including:

- **Aragonese:** Aragonese is a Romance language that is spoken in the central Pyrenees, in the region of Aragon.

- **Gascon:** Gascon is a Romance language that is spoken in the southwestern Pyrenees, in the region of Aquitaine.

- **Aranese:** Aranese is a variety of Occitan that is spoken in the Val d'Aran, a valley in the central Pyrenees.

The languages of the Pyrenees are constantly evolving, and the use of certain languages is declining in some areas. However, there is a growing interest in preserving and promoting the region's linguistic diversity.

In addition to the spoken languages, there are also a number of sign languages used in the Pyrenees. The most widely used sign language in the region is Catalan Sign Language, which is spoken by deaf people in Catalonia, Aragon, and Valencia. There are also a number of regional sign languages, including Occitan Sign Language and Basque Sign Language.

The languages and communication of the Pyrenees are a rich and complex tapestry that reflects the region's history, culture, and geography. The study of the languages of the Pyrenees is a fascinating and rewarding endeavour, and it can help us to better understand the region's past, present, and future.

Transportation in the Pyrenees

The Pyrenees region is home to a variety of transportation options, including:

1. **Train:** There are several train lines that run through the Pyrenees, including the TGV high-speed train. The train is a great way to travel long distances, and it can also be used to access some of the smaller villages in the region.

2. **Bus:** There are also a number of bus lines that operate in the Pyrenees. Buses are a good option for

shorter distances, and they can be more affordable than the train.

3. Car: If you want to have more flexibility in your travels, you can rent a car. Cars are a great way to explore the Pyrenees at your own pace, and they can also be used to access some of the more remote areas of the region.

4. Hiking: If you're looking for a more adventurous way to travel, you can hike through the Pyrenees. There are a number of well-marked trails that lead to some of the most beautiful spots in the region.

5. Biking: Biking is another great way to explore the Pyrenees. There are a number of dedicated bike trails that wind through the mountains, and you can also bike on some of the roads and paths that are used by cars and buses.

The best way to get around the Pyrenees will depend on your individual needs and preferences. If you're looking for a fast and efficient way to travel, the train or bus may be the best option for you. If you want to have more flexibility and explore the region at your own pace, a car or a bike may be a better choice.

Here are some additional tips for transportation in the Pyrenees:

- If you're planning on hiking or biking, be sure to check the weather conditions before you go. The weather in the Pyrenees can change quickly, and it's important to be prepared.
- If you're renting a car, be sure to get a car that is suitable for the terrain. The roads in the Pyrenees can be narrow and winding, and you'll need a car that can handle the hills.

- If you're taking the bus, be sure to check the schedule in advance. Buses in the Pyrenees can be infrequent, and you don't want to get stranded.

Where to Stay

The Pyrenees is home to a variety of accommodation options, to suit all budgets and preferences.

Here are some of the most popular accommodation options in the Pyrenees:

1. Hotels: There are hotels of all sizes and price ranges in the Pyrenees. From small, family-run hotels to luxury resorts, there is sure to be a hotel to suit your needs.

2. Bed and breakfasts: Bed and breakfasts are a great way to experience the local culture and cuisine. Many bed and breakfasts are located in charming villages, and they offer a more personalised experience than a hotel.

3. Gîtes: Gîtes are self-catering accommodations that are often located in rural areas. Gîtes can be a great option for families or groups of friends, as they offer more space and privacy than a hotel room.

4. Camping: Camping is a popular option for budget-minded travellers. There are campsites of all sizes in the Pyrenees, from simple campgrounds with basic facilities to luxury campsites with swimming pools, restaurants, and bars.

5. Chalets: Chalets are a great option for those who want to experience the great outdoors. Chalets can be rented by the week or the month, and they typically come with all the amenities you need for a comfortable stay, including a kitchen, bathroom, and living area.

When choosing accommodation in the Pyrenees, it is important to consider your budget, your preferences, and the activities you plan to do during your stay. If you are on a budget, camping or a hostel may be a good option. If you prefer a more luxurious stay, a hotel or a chalet may be a better choice. And if you are planning on doing a lot of hiking or skiing, you may want to choose an accommodation that is close to the trails or the slopes.

Here are some additional tips for choosing accommodation in the Pyrenees:

• Book your accommodation in advance, especially if you are travelling during the peak season.
• Consider the location of your accommodation. If you want to be close to the action, choose an accommodation in a town or village. If you prefer a

more peaceful stay, choose an accommodation in a rural area.

- Read reviews of different accommodations before you book. This will give you an idea of what to expect.

Title: The Epitome of Luxury: 5 Exquisite Hotels, Resorts, and Chalets in the Pyrenees

Best Luxury Places to Stay

Nestled amidst the breathtaking beauty of the Pyrenees, a mountain range spanning the border between France and Spain, lies a collection of extraordinary accommodations that epitomise luxury and refinement. From world-class hotels to secluded resorts and enchanting chalets, the Pyrenees offers discerning travellers an opportunity to experience a truly opulent retreat. In this article, we present the five best luxury hotels, resorts, and chalets in the Pyrenees, where indulgence meets unparalleled natural beauty.

1. Grand Hôtel du Palais, Biarritz, France:

Situated on the southwestern coast of France, near the Pyrenees, the Grand Hôtel du Palais in Biarritz exudes timeless elegance. This legendary palace hotel, overlooking the Atlantic Ocean, offers sumptuous rooms and suites adorned with lavish decor and stunning sea views. Guests can savour exquisite Michelin-starred dining, unwind in the opulent spa, and enjoy private access to the beach. The Grand Hôtel du Palais ensures a refined experience combined with the region's breathtaking scenery.

2. Hotel Val de Neu, Baqueira-Beret, Spain:

Nestled in the heart of the Spanish Pyrenees, Hotel Val de Neu is a sanctuary of luxury and tranquillity. With its traditional alpine architecture seamlessly blending with modern elegance, this five-star hotel offers exceptional rooms and suites, many featuring private terraces with panoramic mountain views. Guests can indulge in gourmet cuisine, rejuvenate in the deluxe spa, and enjoy seamless access to the renowned Baqueira-Beret ski resort, making it an idyllic retreat for both winter and summer escapes.

3. La Pleta Hotel & Spa, Baqueira-Beret, Spain:

Set against the backdrop of majestic mountains, La Pleta Hotel & Spa in Baqueira-Beret is a haven of sophistication. The property boasts lavish rooms and suites adorned with rustic charm and contemporary design, while the spa offers a wide range of treatments inspired by Pyrenean wellness traditions. Guests can relish Michelin-starred gastronomy, partake in exhilarating outdoor activities, and unwind by the fireplace in this intimate mountain retreat.

4. Chalet Ormello, Val d'Aran, Spain:

Tucked away in the picturesque Val d'Aran, Chalet Ormello is a secluded alpine retreat that redefines luxury chalet living. This exceptional private residence boasts opulent interiors, featuring cozy fireplaces, a private cinema, and a spa area with a swimming pool and sauna. With personalised service, including a private chef and dedicated staff, Chalet Ormello offers an unparalleled experience of exclusivity, surrounded by pristine nature and awe-inspiring mountain vistas.

5. Hotel Les Closes, Andorra la Vella, Andorra:

In the charming capital of the small nation of Andorra, Hotel Les Closes combines elegance with a warm and welcoming atmosphere. This boutique hotel offers well-appointed rooms and suites, tastefully decorated in a contemporary style. Guests can indulge in gourmet cuisine at the hotel's restaurant, explore the nearby Pyrenean landscapes, or indulge in tax-free shopping in Andorra's bustling city centre. Hotel Les Closes offers a perfect balance of luxury, convenience, and cultural exploration.

The Pyrenees region presents an array of luxury accommodations, each offering an enchanting experience of refined hospitality amidst awe-inspiring natural surroundings. Whether you choose the opulence of a grand hotel, the seclusion of a mountain resort, or the intimacy of a luxurious chalet, the Pyrenees promises an unforgettable escape where luxury meets the untamed beauty of the mountains. Embark on a journey of indulgence and relaxation, and let the Pyrenees captivate your senses like never before.

Pyrenees offers not only luxurious accommodations but also an array of affordable options for travellers seeking a budget-friendly retreat. Whether you prefer a cozy bed and breakfast, a charming camping experience, or a comfortable hotel, the Pyrenees has something to suit every traveller's wallet. We present the five best low-budget hotels, campsites, and bed and breakfasts in the Pyrenees, where affordability meets captivating natural beauty.

1. Hotel Les 3 Cimes Blanche, Bagneres-de-Bigorre, France:

Nestled in the picturesque town of Bagneres-de-Bigorre, Hotel Les 3 Cimes Blanche offers comfortable and budget-friendly accommodation. The hotel features clean and cozy rooms with modern amenities, ensuring a pleasant stay. With its convenient location near the Pyrenees National Park, guests can easily explore the region's stunning hiking trails and natural wonders. Hotel Les 3 Cimes Blanche provides excellent value for money without compromising on comfort.

2. Camping La Vallée Heureuse, Argeles-Gazost, France:

For those seeking an immersive camping experience without breaking the bank, Camping La Vallée Heureuse is a perfect choice. Located near Argeles-Gazost, this campsite offers affordable pitches for tents, caravans, and motorhomes. Surrounded by lush greenery and serene landscapes, guests can enjoy a range of amenities, including clean sanitary facilities, a swimming pool, and a communal barbecue area. Camping La Vallée Heureuse is an ideal base for exploring the Pyrenees on a budget.

3. B&B L'Ambassadeur, Lourdes, France:

Situated in the pilgrimage town of Lourdes, B&B L'Ambassadeur offers comfortable and affordable accommodation with a touch of charm. The bed and breakfast features cozy rooms decorated in a traditional style, providing a peaceful retreat for guests. With its close proximity to the Sanctuary of Our Lady of Lourdes and other notable attractions, B&B L'Ambassadeur is a convenient and budget-friendly option for travellers exploring the Pyrenees.

4. Camping Prado Verde, Espot, Spain:

Located in the heart of the Spanish Pyrenees, Camping Prado Verde offers a budget-friendly camping experience surrounded by breathtaking natural beauty. The campsite provides spacious pitches for tents and campervans, as well as cozy wooden cabins for those seeking a bit more comfort. Guests can enjoy outdoor activities such as hiking, fishing, and skiing in the nearby Espot ski resort. Camping Prado Verde is an affordable gateway to the wonders of the Pyrenees.

5. Hostal Escuils, Sort, Spain:

Nestled in the charming town of Sort, Hostal Escuils offers budget-friendly accommodation with a cozy and welcoming atmosphere. The guesthouse provides simple and comfortable rooms, perfect for a restful night's sleep after a day of exploring the Pyrenees. With its central location, guests can easily access various outdoor activities, including rafting, canyoning, and hiking. Hostal Escuils is a wallet-friendly option for those seeking adventure and affordability.

The Pyrenees not only caters to luxury travellers but also provides an array of affordable accommodations for budget-conscious explorers. Whether you choose a budget hotel, a serene campsite, or a charming bed and breakfast, these options offer comfort, convenience, and the opportunity to immerse yourself in the awe-inspiring landscapes of the Pyrenees without breaking the bank. Embrace the beauty of the mountains while keeping your travel expenses in check with these delightful low-budget options in the Pyrenees.

How to Get Cheap Accommodation

While accommodation expenses can add up as you are planning your trip, there are various ways to enjoy your vacation without overspending. In this section, we will explore different strategies to secure cheap accommodation in the Pyrenees, allowing you to fully immerse yourself in the splendour of the mountains while keeping your budget intact.

1. House Sitting: House sitting is an excellent way to score free accommodation while enjoying the comforts of a home away from home. Numerous platforms connect homeowners with trustworthy individuals willing to take care of their properties and pets while they are away. By signing up on these platforms and creating a compelling profile, you can increase your chances of finding a house-sitting opportunity in the Pyrenees.

2. Volunteering: Volunteering is a rewarding way to contribute to the local community while securing free accommodation. Several organisations in the Pyrenees offer opportunities for volunteers to assist with conservation projects, organic farming, or cultural events. In exchange for your time and efforts, you may receive food, lodging, and a chance to connect with the locals and immerse yourself in their way of life.

3. Work Exchanges: Consider participating in work exchanges where you exchange your skills and labour for accommodation. Websites like Workaway, HelpX, and WWOOF (World Wide Opportunities on Organic Farms) connect travellers with hosts who require assistance with various tasks, such as gardening, cooking, or renovation work. These exchanges often provide a place to stay and sometimes include meals, allowing you to experience the Pyrenees while engaging with the local community.

4. Couchsurfing: Couchsurfing is a popular hospitality exchange platform that connects travellers with hosts who offer a spare couch, bed, or room free of charge. The Pyrenees region has an active Couchsurfing community, and by creating a profile and reaching out to potential hosts in advance, you may find welcoming locals willing to accommodate you during your stay. Remember to be respectful, follow the rules, and offer gratitude to your hosts for their hospitality.

5. Outdoor Camping: The Pyrenees are a paradise for outdoor enthusiasts, and camping is an excellent way to fully immerse yourself in nature. Research and identify free or low-cost campsites in the region, which are often located in national parks or designated areas. Make sure you research local laws and secure any required licences. Camping allows you to enjoy the scenic beauty of the Pyrenees while keeping your accommodation costs to a minimum.

6. Homestays and House Exchanges:

Consider exploring homestay opportunities where you can rent a room in a local's home at an affordable rate. Websites like Airbnb, Homestay, and HouseExchange offer various options for travellers seeking unique and budget-friendly accommodation experiences. These platforms provide an opportunity to connect with locals, gain insights into their culture, and enjoy a more personalised stay in the Pyrenees.

Travelling on a budget doesn't mean compromising on the quality of your experience. By exploring these strategies, such as house sitting, volunteering, work exchanges, couchsurfing, camping, homestays, and house exchanges, you can secure free or affordable accommodation while discovering the breathtaking beauty of the Pyrenees. Remember to plan ahead, maintain open communication with hosts, and embrace the unique opportunities that arise from engaging with the local community. Enjoy your budget-friendly adventure in the Pyrenees!

Itinerary Suggestions

It is of great importance to plan your itinerary strategically. Research and plan your itinerary in advance to make the most of your time and avoid unnecessary expenses. Look for free or low-cost attractions near each other to minimise transportation costs and plan activities that align with your interests and budget.

One Week in the Pyrenees

- **Day 1-2:** Start in Toulouse, France, and explore its vibrant culture and historic sites.

- **Day 3-4:** Head to Lourdes, known for its religious significance and stunning landscapes.

- **Day 5-6:** Travel to Andorra, a small principality nestled in the mountains, offering outdoor activities, shopping, and relaxation.

- **Day 7:** End your week in the Pyrenees with a visit to the beautiful town of Cauterets, famous for its thermal baths and hiking trails.

Off the Beaten Path: Hidden gems and lesser-known destinations

- **Day 1-2:** Begin your journey in Ainsa, Spain, a charming mediaeval town surrounded by picturesque landscapes.

- **Day 3-4:** Explore the Ordesa and Monte Perdido National Park, a UNESCO World Heritage Site, known for its stunning canyons and waterfalls.

- **Day 5-6:** Visit the Vall de Boí, home to Romanesque churches and breathtaking mountain scenery.

- **Day 7:** Conclude your trip in Bagnères-de-Luchon, a spa town offering natural hot springs and access to excellent hiking trails.

Family-Friendly Adventures in the Pyrenees

- **Day 1-2:** Start in Font-Romeu, a family-friendly resort town with various outdoor activities, including hiking, biking, and a wildlife park.

- **Day 3-4:** Visit the Animal Park of the Pyrenees in Argelès-Gazost, where kids can observe native animals up close.

- **Day 5-6:** Explore the Caves of Bétharram, an underground labyrinth with impressive rock formations and guided tours suitable for all ages.
- **Day 7:** End your trip in Saint-Lary-Soulan, a vibrant village offering a host of family-friendly activities, including swimming pools, mini-golf, and a tree adventure park.

Outdoor Adventures

- **Day 1: Arrival in Toulouse, France**

- Arrive in Toulouse, the gateway to the Pyrenees.
- Explore the city's historic centre and enjoy its vibrant atmosphere.
- Visit the Cité de l'Espace, a space-themed park and museum.

- **Day 2-3: Hiking in the Cirque de Gavarnie, France**

- Travel to Gavarnie, known for its stunning natural amphitheatre, the Cirque de Gavarnie.
- Embark on a full-day hike to explore the cirque, passing by majestic waterfalls and awe-inspiring cliffs.
- Enjoy breathtaking views of the Gavarnie Falls, one of the highest waterfalls in Europe.

● **Day 4-5: Canyoning in Sierra de Guara, Spain**
- Head to Sierra de Guara Natural Park in Spain, renowned for its canyoning opportunities.
- Join a guided canyoning excursion, navigating through narrow gorges, rappelling down waterfalls, and swimming in crystal-clear pools.
- Experience the thrill of canyoning in stunning natural surroundings.

● **Day 6-7: Mountain Biking in Val d'Aran, Spain**

- Travel to Val d'Aran, a picturesque valley known for its mountain biking trails.
- Rent mountain bikes and explore the extensive network of trails, ranging from gentle paths to challenging singletracks.
- Enjoy the stunning alpine scenery, lush forests, and mountain vistas as you cycle through the region.

- **Day 8-9: Rock Climbing in Riglos, Spain**
- Make your way to Riglos, a renowned rock climbing destination.
- Climb the iconic conglomerate rock formations, such as the famous "Mallos de Riglos."
- Enjoy the rush of vertical ascents and panoramic vistas from the top.

Day 10: Departure
- Depart from the Pyrenees, taking with you unforgettable memories of your outdoor adventure.

- If time allows, make a stop in Andorra, a mountainous principality offering various outdoor activities and shopping opportunities.

These itinerary suggestions are just a starting point, and you can customise them based on your interests, available time, and preferred activities. Whether you prefer a comprehensive tour, off-the-beaten-path exploration, or family-focused adventures or outdoor adventures, the Pyrenees offer a wide range of experiences to create unforgettable memories.

Date	Itinerary

CHAPTER THREE

Where To Visit, What To Do

Exploring the Pyrenees is a captivating adventure that unveils the natural wonders and cultural treasures of this majestic mountain range. Whether you're an outdoor enthusiast, a history buff, or a seeker of tranquillity, the Pyrenees offers a myriad of experiences to suit every traveller's preferences.

On the outdoor front, the Pyrenees boasts an abundance of hiking trails, ranging from leisurely strolls to challenging treks, allowing visitors to immerse themselves in breathtaking landscapes of rugged peaks, lush valleys, and cascading waterfalls. Adventure seekers can also indulge in thrilling activities such as rock climbing, mountain biking, and white-water rafting, making the Pyrenees a playground for adrenaline enthusiasts.

For those with a penchant for history and culture, the Pyrenees region is rich with captivating heritage. Mediaeval towns, fortified castles, and ancient monasteries dot the landscape, providing glimpses into a bygone era. The charming towns of Lourdes, Cauterets, and Biarritz offer cultural experiences, from religious pilgrimage sites to vibrant markets and traditional festivals, showcasing the unique blend of French and Spanish influences.

Moreover, the Pyrenees are a sanctuary for wildlife and nature lovers. The Pyrenees National Park, a UNESCO World Heritage site, shelters a diverse ecosystem, including rare flora and fauna such as the Pyrenean chamois and the bearded vulture. Exploring the park's pristine trails and observing the region's remarkable biodiversity is a treat for nature enthusiasts.

Additionally, the Pyrenees are renowned for their rejuvenating thermal spas and wellness retreats. Nestled amidst tranquil surroundings, these spas offer relaxation and rejuvenation through thermal baths, massages, and holistic therapies, allowing visitors to unwind and revitalise amidst the mountain serenity.

Whether you opt for a winter getaway to experience world-class skiing in Baqueira-Beret or a summer escape to revel in the Pyrenees' scenic beauty, the region caters to all seasons. Each season paints the Pyrenees in a different hue, from snowy peaks in winter to vibrant wildflowers in spring, lush greenery in summer, and golden hues in autumn.

Regions and Highlights

The Pyrenees region is divided between France and Spain, each offering unique highlights and attractions for visitors to explore. Here are some notable regions and their highlights within the Pyrenees:

French Pyrenees

- **Pyrenees National Park**: A sprawling natural reserve with picturesque landscapes, diverse wildlife, and excellent hiking trails, including the iconic GR10 trail.

- **Lourdes:** A renowned pilgrimage site attracting millions of visitors each year, known for its Sanctuary of Our Lady of Lourdes and healing waters.

- **Cauterets:** A charming spa town with thermal baths, stunning waterfalls like Pont d'Espagne, and access to the popular ski resort of Cirque du Lys.

- **Gavarnie:** Home to the spectacular Cirque de Gavarnie, a UNESCO World Heritage site featuring a majestic amphitheatre of towering cliffs and Europe's highest waterfall.

Spanish Pyrenees

- Ordesa and Monte Perdido National Park:
A UNESCO World Heritage site renowned for its dramatic canyons, deep valleys, and the stunning Monte Perdido peak.

- Aigüestortes i Estany de Sant Maurici National Park: Known for its sparkling mountain lakes, rugged peaks, and rich biodiversity, offering excellent hiking and nature-watching opportunities.

- Val d'Aran: A picturesque valley with charming villages, traditional stone architecture, and access to superb ski resorts like Baqueira-Beret.

- Andorra: A small independent principality nestled in the Pyrenees, offering tax-free shopping, ski resorts, and outdoor activities like hiking and mountain biking.

Cross-Border Highlights

- **Col du Tourmalet:** A legendary mountain pass in the Pyrenees, frequently featured in the Tour de France, offering breathtaking views and challenging cycling routes.

- **Canyoning in Sierra de Guara:** Located on the southern side of the Pyrenees, this area is known for its thrilling canyoning experiences, featuring natural water slides, jumps, and rappelling down waterfalls.

- **Mediaeval Towns:** Both French and Spanish Pyrenees are dotted with well-preserved mediaeval towns like Foix, Aínsa, and Jaca, showcasing historic architecture, fortresses, and a glimpse into the region's past.

- **Cirque de Gavarnie:** This UNESCO World Heritage Site is a spectacular natural amphitheatre formed by glaciers. It is home to a number of waterfalls, including the Grande Cascade, which is the highest waterfall in France.

- Pic du Midi de Bigorre: This mountain offers stunning views of the Pyrenees and the surrounding countryside. There is a cable car that takes visitors to the summit, where there is a restaurant, an astronomical observatory, and a variety of hiking trails.

- Vallée d'Ossau: This valley is home to some of the most beautiful scenery in the Pyrenees. It is surrounded by snow-capped peaks, lush forests, and cascading waterfalls. There are also a number of charming villages in the valley, including Laruns and Eaux-Bonnes.

- Parque Nacional de Ordesa y Monte Perdido: This national park is home to a number of stunning canyons, including the Garganta de Escuaín and the Cañón de Añisclo. There are also a number of hiking trails in the park, including the famous GR11 trail.

These are just a few of the many regions and highlights that make the Pyrenees a captivating destination for nature lovers, adventure enthusiasts, history buffs, and those seeking a serene mountain escape. Whether you explore the French or Spanish side, or venture across borders, the Pyrenees promise unforgettable experiences and natural beauty at every turn.

Outdoor Activities and Adventure

The Pyrenees, with its awe-inspiring landscapes and diverse terrain, offers a plethora of thrilling adventures and activities for outdoor enthusiasts. From high-altitude treks to adrenaline-pumping sports, the Pyrenees is a playground that beckons adventure seekers from around the world. Let's explore some of the exciting adventures and activities available in this magnificent mountain range.

1. Hiking and Trekking: The Pyrenees boasts an extensive network of hiking trails catering to all levels of experience. From leisurely walks through lush valleys to challenging multi-day treks across mountain peaks, hikers can revel in the region's natural beauty. Notable routes include the GR10 and GR11, which traverse the entire length of the Pyrenees, offering stunning vistas and encounters with diverse flora and fauna.

2. Skiing and Snowboarding: In winter, the Pyrenees transforms into a winter wonderland, attracting skiers and snowboarders. With numerous ski resorts on both the French and Spanish sides, such as Baqueira-Beret, Grandvalira, and La Mongie, visitors can carve through fresh powder, enjoy well-groomed slopes, and experience a range of winter sports. From beginners to experts, the Pyrenees provides options for all skill levels.

3. Canyoning and Whitewater Rafting: The Pyrenees is a haven for thrill-seekers looking to embrace the power of water. Canyoning allows adventurers to navigate narrow gorges, rappel down waterfalls, jump into crystal-clear pools, and slide down natural rock slides. Whitewater rafting on the region's fast-flowing rivers, such as the Noguera Pallaresa, offers an exhilarating experience as you navigate rapids and enjoy the stunning scenery.

4. Paragliding and Hang Gliding: Soar through the skies and take in the breathtaking panoramas of the Pyrenees with paragliding or hang gliding. Experienced pilots offer tandem flights, allowing even beginners to experience the thrill of flying above the mountain peaks and valleys, providing a unique perspective of the region's beauty.

5. Mountain Biking: The Pyrenees offers an extensive network of mountain biking trails that cater to all skill levels. From gentle routes meandering through picturesque landscapes to challenging downhill trails, bikers can explore the region's diverse terrain. Bike parks, such as Les Angles Bike Park and Vallnord Bike Park, provide adrenaline-pumping descents and freestyle opportunities.

6. Wildlife Watching and Nature Photography:

The Pyrenees is home to a rich variety of wildlife, including the iconic Pyrenean chamois, marmots, bearded vultures, and golden eagles. The Pyrenees are a popular destination for birdwatchers, and over 300 species of birds have been recorded in the region. Wildlife enthusiasts and nature photographers can venture into national parks, such as Ordesa and Monte Perdido National Park, to spot these incredible creatures in their natural habitat and capture stunning photographs.

7. Caving and Spelunking: Explore the hidden depths of the Pyrenees by venturing into its underground world. With an extensive network of caves and grottoes, including Gouffre d'Esparros and Grotte de Niaux, adventurers can navigate winding tunnels, marvel at unique rock formations, and discover underground rivers and chambers.

8. Wellness and Relaxation: For those seeking tranquillity, the Pyrenees offers an array of wellness and relaxation options. Indulge in thermal spas, such as Les Bains du Couloubret and Balneario de Panticosa, where you can soak in warm mineral-rich waters and enjoy rejuvenating treatments, providing a serene retreat amidst the mountains.

Natural Parks and Reserves

The Pyrenees, spanning the border between France and Spain, is blessed with a wealth of natural wonders that are preserved and protected within its national parks and reserves. These pristine landscapes offer visitors the opportunity to immerse themselves in untouched wilderness, witness diverse ecosystems, and appreciate the stunning beauty of the Pyrenees. Let's explore some of the remarkable natural parks and reserves in the region.

1. Pyrenees National Park (France): As the oldest national park in the Pyrenees, Pyrenees National Park is a UNESCO World Heritage site and a paradise for nature lovers. Encompassing over 100,000 hectares, the park showcases a stunning range of landscapes, from snow-capped peaks and glacial valleys to lush meadows and deep canyons. It is home to various endangered species, including the

Pyrenean chamois, brown bears, and bearded vultures. Visitors can explore an extensive network of hiking trails, such as the iconic GR10, and discover awe-inspiring natural treasures like the Cirque de Gavarnie, one of Europe's largest natural amphitheatres.

2. Ordesa and Monte Perdido National Park (Spain): Located in the Spanish Pyrenees, Ordesa and Monte Perdido National Park is another UNESCO World Heritage site, known for its dramatic canyons, towering cliffs, and rugged peaks. The park is centred around Monte Perdido, one of the highest peaks in the Pyrenees. Its valleys are adorned with waterfalls, including the mesmerising Cola de Caballo, and showcase a rich variety of flora and fauna. Hiking trails like the Ordesa Valley route lead visitors to stunning viewpoints and enchanting landscapes, allowing for an unforgettable adventure in the heart of nature.

3. Aigüestortes i Estany de Sant Maurici National Park (Spain): Nestled in the Catalan Pyrenees, Aigüestortes i Estany de Sant Maurici National Park is a haven of sparkling mountain lakes, alpine meadows, and rugged peaks. This park's beauty lies in its more than 200 glacial lakes, known as "estanys," which reflect the surrounding mountains in their crystal-clear waters. Visitors can embark on trails that wind through lush forests, cross charming wooden bridges, and lead to breathtaking viewpoints. The park is also home to an array of wildlife, including the elusive Pyrenean ibex and golden eagles.

4. Néouvielle Nature Reserve (France): Situated in the French Pyrenees, the Néouvielle Nature Reserve is a protected area of outstanding beauty. Known for its high-altitude lakes, called "lacs," this reserve is characterised by a remarkable palette of colours, with turquoise waters contrasting against the rocky landscape. The reserve offers a range of hiking trails that reveal stunning vistas of the lakes and the surrounding peaks. It is a paradise for photographers, nature enthusiasts, and those seeking tranquillity amidst alpine splendour.

5. Posets-Maladeta Natural Park (Spain): Located in the Aragonese Pyrenees, Posets-Maladeta Natural Park is a majestic wilderness encompassing rugged peaks, glaciers, and alpine meadows. It is named after its highest peaks, Posets and Maladeta, which attract mountaineers and hikers from around the world. The park is a habitat for diverse flora and fauna, including chamois, marmots, and rare alpine plants. Its trails lead to pristine lakes, such as the beautiful Ibón de Plan, offering serene settings for picnics and moments of contemplation.

These natural parks and reserves of the Pyrenees are not only gateways to breathtaking landscapes but also crucial sanctuaries for preserving biodiversity and conserving the region's natural heritage.

Hot Springs and Spas

The Pyrenees region is renowned for its natural hot springs and rejuvenating spa experiences. Nestled amidst the stunning mountain landscapes, these hot springs offer a tranquil retreat where visitors can unwind, relax, and indulge in wellness therapies. Let's explore some of the notable hot springs and spa destinations in the Pyrenees.

1. Les Bains du Couloubret, Ax-les-Thermes, France: Located in the charming town of Ax-les-Thermes, Les Bains du Couloubret is a popular thermal spa known for its healing waters. The spa features a variety of indoor and outdoor pools, saunas, steam rooms, and relaxation areas.

Immerse yourself in the warm mineral-rich waters and let the therapeutic properties soothe your body and mind. Les Bains du Couloubret also offers a range of wellness treatments and massages for complete rejuvenation.

2. Balneario de Panticosa, Panticosa, Spain:

Set in the picturesque village of Panticosa, Balneario de Panticosa is a historic thermal spa offering a luxurious retreat in the Spanish Pyrenees. Surrounded by majestic peaks, the spa boasts a collection of thermal pools, each with a different temperature and mineral composition. Relax your muscles, ease tension, and soak in the healing waters as you take in the breathtaking views. Balneario de Panticosa also offers a range of spa treatments, including massages and beauty therapies.

3. Thermes de Luchon, Luchon, France: In the

charming town of Luchon, the Thermes de Luchon

is a renowned thermal spa that has been welcoming visitors for over 200 years. The spa utilises the natural thermal springs of the region, which are known for their mineral content and therapeutic benefits. Enjoy a range of hydrotherapy treatments, including baths, showers, and jet massages, to promote relaxation and well-being. The spa's elegant architecture and serene ambiance add to the overall experience.

4. Termas Baronía de Les, Les, Spain: Located in the peaceful village of Les in the Spanish Pyrenees, Termas Baronía de Les offers a unique hot springs experience. The spa features a series of thermal baths set in outdoor terraces, allowing guests to immerse themselves in the warm waters while surrounded by beautiful mountain scenery. Unwind and let the healing properties of the thermal waters work their magic, promoting relaxation and rejuvenation.

5. Balnéa, Loudenvielle, France: Situated in the idyllic village of Loudenvielle, Balnéa is a modern wellness centre that combines hot springs with a range of spa and relaxation facilities. The complex includes a series of outdoor pools with varying temperatures, hydrotherapy jets, saunas, steam rooms, and relaxation areas. Balnéa offers a holistic experience, allowing visitors to soak in the healing waters while enjoying the stunning natural surroundings.

Cultural Sites and Historical Landmarks

The Pyrenees region is not only blessed with breathtaking natural beauty but also boasts a rich cultural heritage and a wealth of historical landmarks. From mediaeval fortresses and ancient monasteries to charming towns and religious pilgrimage sites, the Pyrenees offers a tapestry of history waiting to be explored.

1. Montsegur Castle, France: Perched on a rocky hilltop, Montsegur Castle is a significant historical site associated with the Cathar movement in the 13th century. This well-preserved fortress served as a stronghold for the Cathars, a religious sect, during the Albigensian Crusade. Visitors can explore the ruins, walk through the castle walls, and learn about the captivating history of this symbolic site.

2. Collegiate Church of St. Bertrand de Comminges, France: Situated in the village of St. Bertrand de Comminges, this magnificent Romanesque church is a testament to the region's religious heritage. The church dates back to the 12th century and features stunning architectural details, including a remarkable Gothic cloister. Visitors can admire the intricate sculptures and soak in the spiritual ambiance of this historical place of worship.

3. Aínsa, Spain: Aínsa is a picturesque mediaeval town nestled in the Spanish Pyrenees. Its well-preserved stone architecture, narrow streets, and mediaeval square make it a charming destination for history enthusiasts. Explore the 11th-century Aínsa Castle, which offers panoramic views of the surrounding landscapes, or wander through the town's old quarter to discover ancient buildings and cultural sites.

4. Lourdes, France: Lourdes is a world-renowned pilgrimage site and a significant destination for religious and cultural tourism. The town gained prominence after the reported apparitions of the Virgin Mary to a young girl in 1858. The Sanctuary of Our Lady of Lourdes attracts millions of pilgrims each year, who come to seek solace and witness the Grotto of Massabielle, where the apparitions occurred. The sanctuary complex includes churches, chapels, and the famous baths believed to possess healing properties.

5. Santa Maria de Ripoll Monastery, Spain: Nestled in the town of Ripoll, this impressive Romanesque monastery has a history dating back over a thousand years. The monastery played a pivotal role in the region's cultural and religious development. Visitors can explore the stunning cloister, the church, and the museum, which houses important historical artefacts and exhibits that shed light on the monastery's past.

6. Jaca Citadel, Spain: Located in Jaca, the Jaca Citadel is a well-preserved military fortification that dates back to the late 16th century. It stands as a testament to the region's strategic importance throughout history. Visitors can wander through the citadel's walls, explore the museum housed within its premises, and learn about the military history of the Pyrenees region.

7. St. Martin du Canigou Abbey, France: Perched on a mountainside in the Canigou Massif, St. Martin du Canigou Abbey is a remote and enchanting monastic complex. Founded in the 11th century, the abbey offers a serene and spiritual experience. Visitors can hike through scenic trails to reach the abbey and admire its simple yet beautiful architecture amidst the tranquil mountain setting.

8. Carcassonne: This city in France is a UNESCO World Heritage Site, and is known for its well-preserved mediaeval city walls. Carcassonne is a popular tourist destination, and is home to a number of historical monuments, including the Château Comtal and the Basilica of Saint-Nazaire.

9. Romanesque Churches of the Vall de Boí:
This group of nine churches in the Spanish Pyrenees are UNESCO World Heritage Sites. The churches were built in the 11th and 12th centuries, and are examples of the Catalan Romanesque style.

10. Camino de Santiago: This pilgrimage route to Santiago de Compostela in Spain passes through the Pyrenees. The Camino de Santiago is a popular hiking trail, and is known for its religious and cultural significance.

11. Fort de Vauban: This series of fortifications in the Pyrenees were built by Sébastien Le Prestre de Vauban, a French military engineer. The forts were built to protect France from Spain, and are an example of Vauban's innovative military engineering.

In addition to these well-known sites, there are also a number of smaller cultural attractions in the Pyrenees. These attractions include museums, art galleries, and historical villages. These smaller attractions offer a more intimate glimpse into the region's culture and history.

These cultural sites and historical landmarks in the Pyrenees region offer a glimpse into the past and the rich tapestry of the region's history. Exploring these sites allows visitors to connect with the cultural heritage, marvel at architectural wonders, and gain a deeper understanding of the people who shaped the Pyrenees over the centuries.

Nightlife and Cultural Experiences

The Pyrenees also offers a vibrant nightlife scene that combines evening entertainment with the charm of the mountains. From lively bars and restaurants to cultural events and music festivals, the Pyrenees has something to suit every taste and mood.

Lively Bars and Restaurants

Many towns and villages in the Pyrenees come alive in the evenings with a variety of bars and restaurants offering a vibrant atmosphere. Whether you're looking for a cozy pub, a trendy cocktail lounge, or a traditional mountain tavern, you'll find a range of establishments to cater to your preferences. Enjoy a refreshing drink, sample local wines, and savour delicious regional cuisine while soaking in the warm and friendly ambiance of the Pyrenees nightlife.

These are just a few of the many lively bars in Pyrenees to have a good time.

1. Le Bateau Ivre in Perpignan. This bar is located in the heart of Perpignan and is known for its lively atmosphere. It has a large outdoor terrace that is perfect for people-watching.

2. La Taverne des Pyrénéens in Cauterets.

This bar is located in the centre of Cauterets and is a popular spot for skiers and snowboarders. It has a large selection of beers on tap and a lively atmosphere.

3. Le Carré in Font-Romeu. This bar is located in the centre of Font-Romeu and is a popular spot for locals and tourists alike. It has a large dance floor and a lively atmosphere.

4. Le Central in Lourdes. This bar is located in the centre of Lourdes and is a popular spot for pilgrims and tourists alike. It has a large selection of beers on tap and a lively atmosphere.

5. Le Pub irlandais in Foix: This bar is located in the centre of Foix and is a popular spot for locals and tourists alike. It has a large selection of Irish beers and a lively atmosphere.

6. Le Saint James in Saint-Lary-Soulan: This bar is located in the centre of Saint-Lary-Soulan and is a popular spot for skiers and snowboarders. It has a large selection of beers on tap and a lively atmosphere.

7. La Distillerie in Argelès-sur-Mer: This bar is located in the centre of Argelès-sur-Mer and is a popular spot for locals and tourists alike. It has a large selection of cocktails and a lively atmosphere.

8. Le Zinc in Collioure: This bar is located in the centre of Collioure and is a popular spot for locals and tourists alike. It has a large selection of wines and a lively atmosphere.

9. La Boîte in Tarbes: This bar is located in the centre of Tarbes and is a popular spot for locals and students alike. It has a large dance floor and a lively atmosphere.

Cultural Events and Festivals

The Pyrenees region hosts a variety of cultural events and festivals throughout the year, providing a unique nightlife experience. From traditional music and dance performances to art exhibitions and theatre productions, there's always something happening to engage and entertain visitors. Keep an eye out for local event calendars to discover concerts, theatre shows, and other cultural happenings that showcase the rich heritage and artistic talents of the region.

1. Carnival de Biarritz: Every February, the town of Biarritz on the French side of the Pyrenees transforms into a carnival extravaganza. Colourful parades, masked revellers, and lively music fill the streets as locals and tourists immerse themselves in the festive atmosphere. The Carnival de Biarritz is a wonderful blend of Basque and French traditions, featuring processions, dances, and the ceremonial burning of "Monsieur Carnaval" to bid farewell to winter.

2. Fête des Fleurs, Luchon: In the picturesque town of Luchon, located in the French Pyrenees, the Fête des Fleurs (Festival of Flowers) takes place in August. The streets come alive with vibrant floral displays, parades, and music. The highlight of the festival is the elaborate flower float procession, where locals showcase their creativity by designing stunning floats adorned with a multitude of colourful blooms.

3. Semana Santa, Jaca: Jaca, a historic town on the Spanish side of the Pyrenees, hosts the renowned Semana Santa (Holy Week) celebration. This religious festival takes place in the week leading up to Easter and is characterised by solemn processions featuring elaborate floats, religious statues, and hooded penitents. The streets of Jaca are filled with locals and visitors, creating a sombre yet captivating atmosphere.

4. Feria de Tarbes: Tarbes, a charming city in southwestern France, welcomes the Feria de Tarbes every July. This lively festival celebrates the Spanish influence in the region, with a focus on the traditions of Andalusia. The streets pulsate with flamenco music, dancing, and the vibrant spectacle of bullfighting. The Feria de Tarbes is a true fusion of cultures, offering visitors a taste of both French and Spanish traditions.

5. Festival de Jazz de Cauterets: For jazz enthusiasts, the Festival de Jazz de Cauterets is a must-visit event. Held annually in July in the French Pyrenees, this music festival brings together renowned jazz musicians from around the world. The picturesque town of Cauterets becomes a hub of melodic improvisation, with concerts held in various venues, including open-air stages against the backdrop of the stunning Pyrenean landscape.

6. Andorra la Vella International Jazz Festival: The capital of the small principality of Andorra, Andorra la Vella, hosts an internationally acclaimed jazz festival. Held in July, the festival features an impressive lineup of jazz artists who grace the stages with their exceptional performances. Visitors can enjoy the melodic tunes and soak up the electric atmosphere of this cosmopolitan event.

7. Summer solstice fire festivals: are held in many villages and towns in the Pyrenees on the night of June 23rd. These festivals celebrate the longest day of the year and the coming of summer. People gather to light bonfires, dance, and sing.

8. La Fête de la Transhumance: is a festival that celebrates the annual migration of sheep and goats from the high mountains to the lower valleys. The festival takes place in different villages in the Pyrenees in July or August. There are typically sheepdog trials, music, and dancing.

9. The Lourdes Festival: is a religious festival that takes place in Lourdes, France, every July. The festival attracts millions of pilgrims from all over the world. There are masses, processions, and other religious events.

Casino Entertainment

If you're feeling lucky or simply enjoy the thrill of gaming, the Pyrenees offers several casinos where you can test your skills and try your luck. Casinos provide an exciting nightlife option with a range of games, including slot machines, poker, blackjack, and roulette. Enjoy the elegant surroundings, indulge in fine dining options, and experience the exhilaration of casino entertainment in the heart of the Pyrenees.

1. Casino Barrière de Luchon (France): Located in the town of Bagnères-de-Luchon, which is situated in the French Pyrenees, the Casino Barrière de Luchon offers a range of gaming options including slot machines, blackjack, roulette, and poker. It also hosts regular entertainment shows and events.

2. Casino de Pau (France): Although not directly in the Pyrenees, the Casino de Pau is situated in the city of Pau, which is located at the foothills of the Pyrenees in southwestern France. The casino features various table games, slot machines, and a poker room. It often hosts live music and other entertainment events.

Music and Dance Venues

Music lovers will find a variety of venues in the Pyrenees where they can enjoy live performances and dance the night away. From small jazz clubs to larger concert halls, the region offers a diverse music scene catering to different genres and tastes. Whether you prefer traditional folk music, rock, jazz, or electronic beats, you can find venues hosting live bands, DJs, and music events that will keep you entertained until the early hours.

Nighttime Outdoor Adventures

For those seeking a different kind of nightlife experience, the Pyrenees also offers nighttime outdoor adventures. Embark on a guided night hike or a moonlit snowshoeing excursion to witness the beauty of the mountains under the starry sky. Some ski resorts even offer nighttime skiing or snowboarding experiences for a unique adrenaline rush after dusk. These adventures allow you to explore the Pyrenees in a whole new light and create unforgettable memories under the moonlit peaks.

It's important to note that the nightlife offerings in the Pyrenees may vary depending on the specific town or village and the time of year. It's always a good idea to check local event listings, ask for recommendations from locals or your accommodation, and embrace the unique nightlife experiences that each place has to offer.

Pyrenees Best Kept Secrets

The Pyrenees are a home to some of the most stunning scenery in Europe, with snow-capped peaks, lush valleys, and pristine lakes. But the Pyrenees are also home to some hidden gems that are off the beaten path.

Here are a few of the Pyrenees' best kept secrets:

1. The Cirque de Gavarnie: This natural amphitheatre is one of the most spectacular sights in the Pyrenees. It is surrounded by towering cliffs and waterfalls, and it is a popular spot for hiking, mountaineering, and rock climbing.

2. The Ordesa National Park: This park is home to some of the most diverse wildlife in the Pyrenees, including bears, wolves, and eagles. In

addition, it's a fantastic location for camping, hiking, and fishing.

3. The Pic du Midi de Bigorre: This mountain offers stunning views of the Pyrenees and the surrounding valleys. There is a cable car that takes you to the summit, and there are also hiking trails that lead up to the top.

4. The Cauterets Valley: This valley is home to a number of thermal springs, making it a popular destination for relaxation and rejuvenation. There are also a number of hiking trails and waterfalls in the valley.

5. The Ossau Valley: This valley is known for its traditional Basque culture and its beautiful scenery. There are a number of hiking trails and villages in the valley, making it a great place to experience the Pyrenees at a slower pace.

These are just a few of the Pyrenees' best kept secrets. If you are looking for a truly unique and unforgettable travel experience, be sure to explore these hidden gems.

In addition to these natural wonders, the Pyrenees are also home to a number of charming villages and towns. These villages offer a glimpse into the region's rich history and culture, and they are a great place to experience the local cuisine.

Shorter Treks Trails in Pyrenees

1. Tour of the Basque Country: This 70-kilometer (43-mile) trek takes in the rolling hills and mountains of the western Pyrenees. It starts in the town of Hendaye, France, and winds its way through the Basque Country, crossing into Spain at several points. The route passes through a variety of landscapes, including forests, farmland, and mountain meadows.

2. Pic du Midi d'Ossau: This 40-kilometer (25-mile) trek takes in the iconic peak of Pic du Midi d'Ossau, a 2,877-meter (9,436-foot) mountain that towers over the valley below. The route starts in the town of Laruns, France, and ascends to the summit of the peak via a series of trails. From the summit, there are stunning views of the surrounding mountains and valleys.

3. Tour de Vignemale and La Alta Ruta de Los Perdidos: This 120-kilometer (75-mile) trek is the longest of the shorter treks in the Pyrenees. It takes in the alpine terrain around the Vignemale massif, including the summit of Vignemale, the highest mountain in the French Pyrenees. The route crosses into Spain and passes through the Ordesa y Monte Perdido National Park, a UNESCO World Heritage Site.

4. Réserve Naturelle de Néouvielle: This 50-kilometer (31-mile) trek takes in the beautiful lakes and mountains of the Réserve Naturelle de Néouvielle, a nature reserve in the French Pyrenees. The route starts in the town of Saint-Lary-Soulan and passes through a series of lakes, including Lac d'Aumar and Lac de Bastan. The route also offers stunning views of the surrounding peaks, including Pic du Midi de Bigorre.

5. Carros de Foc: This 53-kilometer (33-mile) trek is a loop trail that takes in the peaks and valleys of the Vall d'Aran in the Spanish Pyrenees. The route passes through a series of mountain refuges, where hikers can stay overnight. The trail is

challenging but offers stunning views of the
surrounding mountains.

6. Scramble up to summit of Canigou: This
8-kilometer (5-mile) trek takes in the summit of
Canigou, the highest mountain in the Catalan
Pyrenees. The route starts in the village of
Vernet-les-Bains and ascends to the summit via a
series of steep trails. The summit offers stunning
views of the surrounding mountains and the
Mediterranean Sea.

7. Pico Tebarrai above Ibón de Tebarrai:
This 10-kilometer (6.2-mile) trek takes in the
beautiful scenery of the Ordesa y Monte Perdido
National Park. The route starts in the village of Torla
and ascends to the summit of Pico Tebarrai, a peak
with stunning views of the surrounding mountains
and valleys.

8. N face, Vignemale from Oulètes de Gaube: This 12-kilometer (7.5-mile) trek takes in the north face of Vignemale, the highest mountain in the French Pyrenees. The route starts in the village of Cauterets and ascends to the Oulètes de Gaube, a series of lakes at the foot of the north face. From the Oulètes de Gaube, hikers can continue to the summit of Vignemale, but this requires some scrambling.

9. Chemin de la Mâture: This 15-kilometer (9.3-mile) trek takes in the spectacular scenery of the Cirque de Gavarnie, a UNESCO World Heritage Site. The route starts in the town of Gavarnie and ascends to the top of the Cirque, where there are stunning views of the surrounding peaks and waterfalls.

CHAPTER FOUR

Towns and Villages

Nestled amidst the majestic mountain ranges, the Pyrenees is home to a collection of picturesque towns and villages that exude charm, history, and a unique local flavour. These idyllic settlements offer a glimpse into traditional mountain life, showcasing stunning architecture, captivating landscapes, and warm hospitality. Let's explore some of the enchanting towns and villages that grace the Pyrenees region.

Cauterets, France

Tucked away in the French Pyrenees, Cauterets is a charming spa town renowned for its natural beauty and thermal baths. The town features elegant Belle Époque architecture, narrow streets, and a bustling town centre. Visitors can explore the historic Casino, relax in the thermal spas, and take in the breathtaking waterfalls of Pont d'Espagne. Cauterets also serves as a gateway to the nearby ski resort of Cirque du Lys, offering year-round outdoor activities.

Boltaña, Spain

Nestled on the banks of the Ara River, Boltaña is a delightful village in the Spanish Pyrenees. Its well-preserved mediaeval centre, cobbled streets, and stone houses create a charming ambiance. Visitors can explore the 16th-century Collegiate Church of San Pedro, wander along the riverfront promenade, and enjoy traditional Aragonese cuisine in local restaurants. Boltaña also serves as a base for outdoor activities, such as hiking, rafting, and canyoning in the surrounding natural wonders.

Saint-Lary-Soulan, France

Perched in the heart of the French Pyrenees, Saint-Lary-Soulan is a picturesque mountain village known for its authentic Pyrenean atmosphere. The village features traditional chalet-style architecture, narrow streets, and cozy cafes. In the winter, it becomes a popular ski destination with access to the extensive Saint-Lary ski area. In the summer, visitors can explore the surrounding hiking trails, visit the nearby Néouvielle Nature Reserve, or simply soak in the laid-back ambiance of this mountain retreat.

Aínsa, Spain

Aínsa is a mediaeval gem located in the Spanish Pyrenees. Its well-preserved stone buildings, narrow streets, and impressive Plaza Mayor create a captivating atmosphere. Visitors can explore the 11th-century Aínsa Castle, wander through the old quarter with its charming shops and restaurants, and enjoy panoramic views of the surrounding landscapes. Aínsa is also a gateway to the Ordesa and Monte Perdido National Park, offering stunning natural beauty and outdoor adventures.

Bagnères-de-Luchon, France

Known as the "Queen of the Pyrenees," Bagnères-de-Luchon is a historic spa town nestled in a beautiful valley. It boasts elegant architecture, grand hotels, and beautiful parks. Visitors can soak in the thermal baths, stroll along the lively promenade, and explore the historic Casino. Bagnères-de-Luchon is also a popular base for outdoor activities, including hiking, cycling, and skiing in the nearby Superbagnères ski resort.

Other Pyrenean towns and villages includes;

1. Puigcerdà, Spain: Puigcerdà is a charming town located in the Cerdanya region of the Spanish Pyrenees. It offers a mix of Catalan and French influences, reflected in its architecture and cultural traditions. Visitors can explore the town's historic centre, enjoy a leisurely stroll around the picturesque lake, and savour the local cuisine in traditional restaurants. Puigcerdà also serves as a gateway to numerous outdoor activities, including hiking, mountain biking, and skiing.

2. Gavarnie: This village in France is located in the heart of the Pyrenees National Park, and is known for its stunning scenery. Gavarnie is home to the Cirque de Gavarnie, a UNESCO World Heritage Site.

3. Andorra la Vella: This capital of Andorra is a small town located in the Pyrenees mountains. Andorra la Vella is a popular tourist destination, and is home to a number of historical monuments, including the Casa de la Vall, the seat of the Andorran government.

These towns and villages of the Pyrenees region captivate visitors with their old-world charm, stunning natural surroundings, and a genuine sense of local hospitality.

CHAPTER FIVE

Local Cuisine and Gastronomy

Welcome to the Pyrenees, where culinary traditions and gastronomic delights abound. The local cuisine of the Pyrenees is a delightful blend of influences from both Spain and France, resulting in a unique and flavorful experience for food enthusiasts.

In this picturesque region, you will discover a wide array of dishes that celebrate the bounties of the mountains, forests, and streams. Traditional Pyrenean cuisine emphasises hearty and rustic flavours, often using locally sourced ingredients to create wholesome and satisfying meals.

One of the prominent features of Pyrenean gastronomy is its reliance on high-quality meats. The mountains are home to numerous grazing animals, including cows, sheep, and pigs, which contribute to the region's exceptional charcuterie and meat-based dishes. Cured hams, sausages, and terrines are crafted with meticulous care, reflecting the artisanal expertise passed down through generations.

Cheese lovers will also find themselves in culinary paradise in the Pyrenees. This mountainous region boasts an impressive range of delectable cheeses, each with its distinct flavours and textures. From the creamy Ossau-Iraty to the pungent Roquefort, cheese connoisseurs can indulge in a captivating journey through the Pyrenean fromageries.

With its close proximity to the sea, the Pyrenees offer an abundance of fresh seafood. Coastal towns along the French and Spanish sides of the range provide an assortment of delicacies such as grilled fish, seafood stews, and shellfish platters. These coastal flavours blend harmoniously with the mountain cuisine, creating a unique fusion of land and sea.

Additionally, the Pyrenees are known for their rich agricultural heritage, evident in the wide variety of fresh produce available. The region's fertile valleys yield an array of seasonal fruits, vegetables, and aromatic herbs that contribute to the vibrant flavours of local dishes. From earthy wild mushrooms to sweet summer berries, the Pyrenean cuisine celebrates the natural bounty of the land.

To accompany these mouthwatering dishes, the Pyrenees offer an extensive selection of wines. On the French side, you can savour robust red wines, such as Madiran or Cahors, while on the Spanish side, the region of Somontano produces elegant whites and fruity reds.

Whether you're exploring the charming villages or venturing into the mountains, the Pyrenees captivate both nature enthusiasts and food lovers alike. Prepare to immerse yourself in a culinary journey that showcases the region's diverse flavours, time-honoured traditions, and a harmonious blend of French and Spanish influences.

Traditional Pyrenean Dishes

The Pyrenees region is home to a rich and varied cuisine, influenced by the different cultures that have settled in the area over the centuries. Some of the most traditional Pyrenean dishes include:

1. Cassoulet: This hearty dish is a stew made with white beans, pork (such as sausages, pork belly, and confit), and sometimes duck or lamb. It is a beloved dish in the Pyrenees region, particularly in the southwestern part of France.

2. Garbure: A traditional Pyrenean soup, garbure is made with cabbage, various vegetables, and often includes ham or other cured meats. It is a filling and flavorful dish commonly enjoyed during the colder months.

3. Trinxat: Hailing from the Catalan Pyrenees, trinxat is a simple but delicious dish made with mashed potatoes, cabbage, and bacon. It can be served on the side or a main course.

4. Axoa: Originating from the Basque region of the Pyrenees, axoa is a flavorful dish made with braised veal or beef, peppers, onions, and Espelette pepper. It is often served with rice or potatoes.

5. Piperade: This Basque dish is a mixture of tomatoes, peppers, and onions, often with the addition of ham or sausage. It is often served on the side or as an appetiser.

6. Fabada: This Asturian stew is made with beans, sausage, and pork. It is a hearty and filling dish that is perfect for a cold day.

7. Picadillo: This Catalan dish is a mixture of ground meat, onions, peppers, and spices. It is mostly served with potatoes or rice.

8. Ragoût: This stew is made with a variety of meats, vegetables, and spices. It is a popular dish in the Pyrenees, and there are many different variations.

Popular Local Ingredients

The Pyrenees region is home to a variety of delicious and unique ingredients, including:

1. Sheep's Milk Cheese: The Pyrenees region is renowned for its excellent sheep's milk cheeses, such as Ossau-Iraty, Roncal, and Val d'Aspe. These cheeses have a distinct flavour and are often enjoyed on their own or as part of various dishes.

2. Game Meat: Due to its mountainous terrain, the Pyrenees offers a wide variety of game meats like wild boar, deer, and mountain goat. These meats are used in stews, sausages, and other traditional dishes.

3. Trout: The Pyrenean rivers and lakes are home to delicious freshwater trout. They are often cooked simply, grilled or pan-fried, and served with local herbs and butter.

4. Wild Mushrooms: The forests of the Pyrenees are a haven for mushroom lovers. Varieties like cèpes, chanterelles, and morel mushrooms are foraged and incorporated into various dishes, adding a rich earthy flavour.

4. Foie gras: This decadent spread is made from the liver of a goose or duck that has been specially fattened. It is a popular ingredient in many Pyrenean dishes.

5. Jamon Iberico: This prized ham is made from Iberian pigs that are fed a diet of acorns and other nuts. It has a rich and nutty flavour that is perfect for charcuterie boards or sandwiches.

6. Txakoli: This slightly sparkling white wine is made in the Basque Country. It is a refreshing and versatile wine that can be enjoyed on its own or with food.

7. Etorki: This sheep's milk cheese is made in the Pyrenees. It has a mild and sweet flavour that is perfect for snacking or serving with fruit.

8. Garlic: Garlic is a popular ingredient in Pyrenean cuisine, and it is often used to flavour meats, vegetables, and sauces.

Notable Restaurants and Food Experiences

There are many great restaurants in the Pyrenees that offer traditional Pyrenean cuisine. Here are a few of the most notable:

1. Can Jubany (Calldetenes, Catalonia, Spain): Located at the eastern edge of the Pyrenees, Can Jubany is a renowned Michelin-starred restaurant run by Chef Nandu Jubany. It offers innovative and refined Catalan cuisine, showcasing local ingredients with a modern twist.

2. Chez Camille (Les Cabannes, Midi-Pyrénées, France): Nestled in the French

Pyrenees, Chez Camille is a charming restaurant known for its traditional Pyrenean dishes. They specialise in hearty stews, local cheeses, and game meats.

3. La Table d'Aurore (Saint-Lary-Soulan, Occitanie, France): Situated in the heart of the Pyrenees, La Table d'Aurore offers a delightful dining experience with a focus on regional cuisine. They serve dishes prepared with local ingredients, including mountain cheeses and game meats.

4. Le Canard: This restaurant in Lourdes is known for its classic Pyrenean dishes, such as cassoulet and piperade.

5. La Maison Rose: This restaurant in Argelès-Gazost is a popular spot for traditional Catalan cuisine.

6. Le Bistrot: This restaurant in Saint-Lary-Soulan offers a mix of traditional and modern Pyrenean cuisine.

7. L'Auberge: This restaurant in Cauterets is a great place to try local specialities, such as foie gras and txakoli.

8. La Creperie: This crêperie in Gavarnie is a great place to enjoy a traditional Pyrenean dessert, such as crêpes with chocolate or fruit.

In addition to restaurants, there are also many other great food experiences to be had in the Pyrenees. Here are a few ideas:

• Take a cooking class: Learn how to make some of your favourite Pyrenean dishes from a local chef.
• Visit a farmers market: Sample fresh, local produce and other ingredients.

• Go on a food tour: Visit different restaurants and food producers in the region.

• Attend a food festival: There are many food festivals held in the Pyrenees throughout the year.

CHAPTER SIX

Practical Tips and Safety Information

These tips are meant to provide general guidance, and it's always advisable to research and adhere to specific safety recommendations and regulations provided by local authorities in the Pyrenees. Stay informed, be prepared, and enjoy your time exploring the breathtaking beauty of the region while prioritising your safety and the well-being of others.

Health and Safety Considerations

• It's advisable to have travel insurance that covers medical expenses and emergency evacuation.

• Carry any necessary medications and prescriptions with you, ensuring you have an ample supply for the duration of your stay.

- Stay hydrated, especially when engaging in outdoor activities, as the mountainous terrain can be physically demanding.
- Be cautious when hiking or engaging in outdoor adventures, and follow safety guidelines and recommendations from local authorities.
- Check weather conditions and be prepared for changes in temperature, especially if you plan to explore higher altitudes.
- Respect wildlife and nature conservation efforts, and avoid feeding or approaching wild animals.
- Be sure to have a first-aid kit with you. This is especially important if you are planning on hiking or camping in the Pyrenees.

Local Customs and Etiquette

- The Pyrenees region encompasses both French and Spanish cultures, so it's important to be aware of and respect the local customs of the specific area you're visiting.

- Greetings are generally accompanied by a handshake or a kiss on both cheeks, depending on the cultural norms of the location.

- Politeness and courtesy are highly valued, so remember to say "please" (s'il vous plaît in French, por favour in Spanish) and "thank you" (merci in French, gracias in Spanish) when interacting with locals.

- Dress appropriately when visiting religious sites and adhere to any specific dress codes.

- It's customary to tip in restaurants and cafes, usually around 5-10% of the total bill, unless a service charge is already included.

Important Contact Information

- Emergency services: Dial 112 for emergency assistance in both France and Spain.
- Tourist information: 0810 123 123
- Medical services: 15
- Police: 17

- Fire: 18
- Local authorities: Familiarise yourself with the contact information for local police stations, hospitals, and embassies or consulates of your home country.

Packing List for the Pyrenees

Winter

When visiting the Pyrenees in the winter season, it's important to pack appropriately to stay warm and comfortable in the cold weather. Here are some essential items you should consider packing:

1. Warm Clothing: Pack thermal base layers, including long-sleeved tops and leggings, to keep your body insulated. Bring sweaters, fleece jackets, and warm pants for layering. Don't forget to pack thermal socks, gloves, and a beanie or hat to protect your extremities.

2. Waterproof Outerwear: The Pyrenees experience snowfall in winter, so pack a waterproof and insulated winter coat or jacket. Look for a jacket with a hood to shield yourself from snow and wind. Waterproof pants or snow pants are also recommended.

3. Footwear: Choose sturdy and waterproof boots with good traction to navigate snowy or icy terrain. Insulated boots or those with removable liners will provide extra warmth. Pack extra pairs of warm socks.

4. Accessories: Bring a scarf or neck gaiter to protect your neck and face from cold winds. Consider packing hand warmers or heating pads for added comfort. Sunglasses and sunscreen are also essential to protect your eyes and skin from glare and UV rays.

5. Snow Gear: If you plan to engage in winter activities like skiing or snowboarding, pack or rent appropriate equipment, such as skis, snowboards, boots, poles, and helmets. Don't forget to bring your goggles for eye protection.

6. Layers: Pack multiple layers of clothing to adjust your insulation based on the temperature. This allows you to add or remove layers as needed to maintain a comfortable body temperature.

7. Backpack: A sturdy backpack is useful for carrying extra clothing, snacks, water, and any other essentials you may need during your outdoor adventures.

8. First Aid Kit: It's always a good idea to carry a basic first aid kit with supplies like bandages, pain relievers, blister treatment, and any necessary medication.

9. Navigation Tools: If you plan to explore the wilderness or hike in the Pyrenees, bring a map, compass, or GPS device to ensure you can navigate safely.

10. Camera: The Pyrenees offer stunning winter landscapes, so don't forget your camera or smartphone to capture memorable moments.

Remember to check the weather forecast before your trip to give an idea of what to pack or not. Dressing in layers will give you the flexibility to adjust your clothing to changing weather conditions. Stay safe and enjoy your visit to the beautiful Pyrenees in winter!

Summer

When visiting the Pyrenees in summer, it's important to pack appropriately to ensure you have a comfortable and enjoyable trip. Here are some essential items to include in your packing list:

1. Clothing:

- Lightweight, breathable clothing: T-shirts, shorts, and skirts for warm weather.

- Long-sleeved shirts and pants for cooler evenings and protection against insects.

- Comfortable hiking or walking shoes with good traction.

- Light rain jacket or windbreaker.

- Swimsuit and towel if you plan to swim in lakes or rivers.

- sunglasses, hats, and sunscreen for protection from the ultraviolet rays from the sun.

- A lightweight sweater or fleece for cooler temperatures at higher altitudes.

2. Outdoor Gear:

- Daypack for carrying water, snacks, and other essentials during hikes.

- Hiking boots or sturdy walking shoes for more challenging terrain.

- Trekking poles for additional stability during hikes.

- Water can or hydration bladder to enable you to stay hydrated during your adventure.

- Insect repellent to protect against mosquitoes and other bugs.

- Binoculars for wildlife observation.

3. Safety and Navigation:

- Detailed map and this guidebook of the Pyrenees region.

- Compass or GPS device for navigation.

- Whistle for signalling in case of emergencies.

- First aid kit with essential supplies like band-aids, pain relievers, and antiseptic.

- Personal medication, if required.

4. Miscellaneous Items:

- Camera or smartphone for capturing the stunning landscapes.

- Power bank or extra batteries for electronic devices.

- Travel adapter if you're visiting from a different country.

- Lightweight travel towel for convenience.

- Cash or credit cards for purchases and emergencies.

- Snacks and energy bars for hikes and long days outdoors.

- Travel insurance information and important documents.

Remember to check the weather forecast for the specific region and time of your visit to the Pyrenees and adjust your packing list accordingly.

Additionally, it's always a good idea to consult local resources or experienced hikers for any specific recommendations or requirements based on your planned activities and destinations within the Pyrenees.

Useful Phrases in the Local Language

French

Here are some useful French phrases for someone visiting the Pyrenees:

1. Greetings:

- Hello: Bonjour
- Good evening: Bonsoir
- Goodbye: Au revoir

2. Basic Communication:

- Yes: Oui
- No: Non

- Please: S'il vous plaît

- Thank you: Merci

- You're welcome: De rien

- Excuse me: Excusez-moi

- I'm sorry: Je suis désolé(e)

- I don't understand: Je ne comprends pas

3. Directions and Assistance:

- Where is...?: Où est...?

- Can you help me?: Pouvez-vous m'aider?

- I'm lost: Je suis perdu(e)

- Could you please repeat that?: Pouvez-vous répéter, s'il vous plaît?

4. Ordering Food and Drinks:

- I would like...: Je voudrais...

- What do you recommend?: Qu'est-ce que vous recommandez?

- The bill, please: L'addition, s'il vous plaît

- Do you have a menu in English?: Avez-vous un menu en anglais?

5. Transportation:

- Where is the nearest bus/train station?: Où est la gare routière/ferroviaire la plus proche?
- How much does a ticket cost?: Combien coûte un billet?
- When does the bus/train leave?: Quand est-ce que le bus/train part?
- Where can I find a taxi?: Où puis-je trouver un taxi?

6. Emergency Situations:

- Help!: À l'aide!
- I need a doctor: J'ai besoin d'un médecin
- Where is the hospital?: Où est l'hôpital?
- Call the police: Appelez la police

7. Polite Phrases:

- Excuse me, do you speak English?: Excusez-moi, parlez-vous anglais?

- Could you please help me?: Pourriez-vous m'aider, s'il vous plaît?

- I'm sorry, I don't speak French very well: Je suis désolé(e), je ne parle pas très bien français.

Learning a few basic French phrases can greatly enhance your experience in the Pyrenees and help you communicate with locals. Don't hesitate to use these phrases and show your willingness to engage with the local culture and language.

Spanish

1. Greetings:

- Hello: Hola
- Good morning: Buenos días
- Good afternoon: Buenas tardes
- Good evening: Buenas noches

2. Basic Phrases:

- Thank you: Gracias
- Please: Por favour
- Yes: Sí
- No: No
- Excuse me: Perdón or Disculpe
- I'm sorry: Lo siento
- Do you speak English?: ¿Hablas inglés?
- I don't understand: No entiendo
- Can you help me?: ¿Puedes ayudarme?

3. Directions and Transportation:

- Where is...?: ¿Dónde está...?
- How do I get to...?: ¿Cómo llego a...?
- Is it far?: ¿Está lejos?
- How much does it cost?: ¿Cuánto cuesta?
- Where is the nearest bus/train station?: ¿Dónde está la estación de autobuses/tren más cercana?

- Where can I find a taxi?: ¿Dónde puedo encontrar un taxi?

4. Dining and Food:

- I would like...: Me gustaría...
- What do you recommend?: ¿Qué recomiendas?
- Can I see the menu, please?: ¿Puedo ver el menú, por favor?
- I'm vegetarian/vegan: Soy vegetariano(a)/vegano(a)
- The bill, please: La cuenta, por favor
- Cheers!: ¡Salud!

5. Emergencies:

- Help!: ¡Ayuda!
- I need a doctor: Necesito un médico
- Where is the hospital?: ¿Dónde está el hospital?
- Call the police: Llame a la policía
- I lost my passport: Perdí mi pasaporte

Remember, making an effort to communicate in the local language can go a long way in connecting with the locals and enhancing your travel experience in the Pyrenees.

Money Saving Tips and Local Insights

1. Travel during the shoulder seasons: Consider visiting the Pyrenees during the spring or autumn months. Not only will you enjoy milder weather and fewer crowds, but you'll also find more affordable accommodations and travel deals compared to the peak summer and winter seasons.

2. Stay in budget-friendly accommodations: Look for guesthouses, hostels, or campsites instead of upscale hotels. These options not only offer more affordable rates but also provide opportunities to interact with locals and fellow travellers.

3. Cook your meals: Save money on dining out by preparing some of your meals yourself. Consider staying in accommodations with kitchen facilities or opt for picnics in scenic locations. Visit local markets to buy fresh produce, cheese, and other local specialties, and enjoy a budget-friendly meal with a view.

4. Take advantage of free attractions and activities: The Pyrenees offer a wealth of natural beauty and cultural sites that you can explore for free. Enjoy scenic hikes, visit public parks, explore charming villages, and take in the stunning landscapes without spending a dime.

5. Utilise public transportation: Public transportation options like buses and trains are often more affordable than renting a car. Research local transportation schedules and consider using regional passes or cards for discounted fares. Additionally, many areas offer hiking shuttles or cable cars for accessing remote hiking trails and mountain top viewpoints.

6. Opt for local experiences: Engage in local activities and events to get a more authentic and budget-friendly experience. Attend local festivals, explore small villages, and participate in free or low-cost outdoor activities like nature walks or guided tours led by local experts.

7. Research discount passes and cards: Look for regional or city-specific discount passes that offer discounted entry fees to attractions, public transportation, or even bundled activity packages. These passes can help you save money while enjoying a range of experiences.

8. Pack appropriately: Bring along items that can help you save money, such as a reusable water bottle to refill at water fountains or natural springs, a picnic blanket for outdoor meals, and a backpack for carrying snacks and essentials during hikes.

9. Connect with locals: Engage with locals to gain insights into affordable dining options, hidden gems, and local tips. They can recommend budget-friendly restaurants, lesser-known hiking trails, or free local events happening during your visit.

10. Plan your itinerary strategically: Research and plan your itinerary in advance to make the most of your time and avoid unnecessary expenses. Look for free or low-cost attractions near each other to minimise transportation costs and plan activities that align with your interests and budget.

By incorporating these money-saving tips and local insights, you can have a memorable and budget-friendly trip to the Pyrenees without compromising on the beauty and experiences this region has to offer.

CHAPTER SEVEN

Appendix

As you embark on your Pyrenees adventure, it's crucial to have access to essential information that can enhance your trip and ensure a smooth and enjoyable experience.

Additional Resources and Websites

When visiting the Pyrenees, there are several additional resources you can utilise to enhance your trip and make the most of your experience. Here are some recommendations:

1. Official Tourism Websites: Visit the official tourism websites of the countries that the Pyrenees spain, such as France and Spain. These websites provide comprehensive information about the region, including attractions, activities, accommodations, and events. Examples include:

- French Pyrenees Tourism: https://www.pyrenees.fr/
- Visit Spain Pyrenees: https://www.spain.info/en/destination/pyrenees/

2. Local Visitor Centers: Once you arrive in the Pyrenees, stop by local visitor centres or tourist offices. They can provide you with maps, brochures, and valuable advice about the best places to visit, hiking trails, local events, and any current updates or restrictions.

3. Hiking and Outdoor Guides: There are numerous guidebooks and online resources specifically focused on hiking and outdoor activities in the Pyrenees.

4. Online Forums and Travel Communities: Joining online forums and travel communities dedicated to the Pyrenees can provide you with

valuable insights, tips, and recommendations from fellow travellers who have already visited the region. Platforms like TripAdvisor, Lonely Planet's Thorn Tree forum, and Reddit's r/travel or r/hiking can be excellent sources of information.

5. Local Guides and Tour Operators: If you prefer guided experiences, consider hiring a local guide or joining organised tours. They can offer in-depth knowledge, take you to off-the-beaten-path locations, and ensure your safety during outdoor activities. Look for reputable guides or tour operators specialising in the Pyrenees region.

Useful Mobile Apps

When visiting the Pyrenees, there are several useful mobile apps that can enhance your experience and assist you during your trip. Here are some recommended apps:

1. AllTrails: This popular app provides a vast collection of hiking and trail maps, along with user reviews and photos. It offers detailed information about trails in the Pyrenees, including difficulty levels, distances, elevation profiles, and offline maps. You can also track your progress and record your hikes using GPS.

2. PeakFinder: With this app, you can identify mountain peaks in the Pyrenees and gain panoramic views using augmented reality technology. It provides information about the names and altitudes of surrounding peaks, helping you navigate and appreciate the stunning landscape.

3. GeoRando: GeoRando offers detailed topographic maps and GPS tracking for outdoor activities. It covers a wide range of hiking trails in the Pyrenees and provides information about waypoints, distances, elevations, and estimated completion times. The app also works offline, which is useful in areas with limited or no internet connectivity.

4. Pyrénées 2 Vallées: This app focuses specifically on the Pyrénées 2 Vallées region, covering resorts, hiking trails, mountain biking routes, and tourist attractions. It provides real-time information on ski conditions, lifts, weather, and events. You can also find nearby accommodations, restaurants, and services.

5. Pyrénées Andorra: If you're visiting the Andorran side of the Pyrenees, this app offers comprehensive information about the region. It provides details about ski resorts, hiking trails, activities, shopping, accommodations, and dining options. You can also access real-time weather updates and interactive maps.

6. Weather Apps: Having a reliable weather app is essential when exploring the Pyrenees. Consider downloading apps like AccuWeather, Weather Underground, or The Weather Channel to get accurate forecasts, including temperature, precipitation, wind speed, and sunrise/sunset times.

7. Viewranger: is a free GPS and digital mapping app with excellent free, downloadable, hiking maps for the Pyrenees and all over the world. It works offline, so you don't need a data package or mobile coverage. This is a great app for hiking, biking, and trail running.

8. Gaia GPS: is another great GPS and mapping app with offline maps for the Pyrenees. It also has a lot of features for hiking, biking, and camping, such as the ability to track your progress, create waypoints, and download custom maps.

9. Lourdes Pyrenees City Card: is a mobile app that provides information on all the partners of the Lourdes Pyrenees City Card, including museums, restaurants, and attractions. You can also use the app to book activities and get discounts on your purchases.

10. Pyrenees Mountain Weather: is a weather app that provides detailed forecasts for the Pyrenees. It includes information on temperature, precipitation, wind, and snow conditions.

11. Pyrenees Flora and Fauna: is an app that identifies plants and animals in the Pyrenees. It has a database of over 10,000 species, and you can use it to learn about the plants and animals you see during your travels.

12. Maps.me: is a free offline maps app that provides detailed maps of the Pyrenees and other parts of the world. It also has a built-in GPS, so you can track your location and get directions even when you don't have cell service.

13. Couchsurfing: is a great app for meeting locals and finding free accommodation in the Pyrenees. It's a great way to learn about the local culture and make new friends.

14. Duolingo: is a great app for learning the local language, French or Spanish. It's a fun and interactive way to learn new vocabulary and grammar.

15. TripAdvisor: is a great app for finding restaurants, hotels, and attractions in the Pyrenees. It has user reviews and ratings, so you can make sure you're choosing the best places to visit.

Remember to download and familiarise yourself with these apps before your trip to ensure that you have access to the necessary maps and information, especially if you anticipate being in areas with limited internet connectivity. Always prioritise your safety and be aware of your surroundings while using mobile apps in outdoor settings.

Remember to always stay informed about any local regulations, weather conditions, and potential hazards before embarking on any outdoor activities in the Pyrenees. Being well-prepared and informed will ensure a safe and enjoyable trip.

Exploring Pyrenees on a Budget

Exploring the Pyrenees on a budget can be an incredibly rewarding experience. Here are some tips to make the most of your trip while keeping costs in check:

1. Plan your trip during the shoulder seasons: Consider visiting the Pyrenees during the spring or fall when tourist crowds are thinner, and accommodation prices are generally lower.

2. Choose budget-friendly accommodations:
Look for affordable options such as guesthouses, hostels, or campsites in smaller towns and villages instead of staying in expensive resorts or hotels in popular tourist destinations.

3. Take advantage of public transportation:
Utilise local buses, trains, or shared taxis to get around the Pyrenees. Public transportation is often cheaper than renting a car and allows you to enjoy the scenic routes without the hassle of driving.

4. Pack your own meals: Save money on food by preparing your own meals. Visit local markets or grocery stores to buy fresh produce, bread, and local specialties for picnics or cooking in shared kitchens at accommodations.

5. Explore the natural wonders: The Pyrenees offer an abundance of natural beauty that can be enjoyed for free or at a minimal cost. Take advantage of hiking trails, picnic spots, and scenic viewpoints to immerse yourself in the stunning landscapes without spending a fortune.

6. Research free or discounted attractions: Look for free or discounted entry days to museums, cultural sites, and attractions in the Pyrenees. Many places offer reduced rates during certain times or for specific groups, such as students or seniors.

7. Join group activities or tours: Consider joining group activities or guided tours, as they often offer shared costs and can be more affordable than individual bookings. Look for options like group hiking trips, wildlife excursions, or cultural tours and you can also find most of these groups on social media platforms.

8. Connect with locals: Engage with locals to get insider tips on budget-friendly experiences, hidden gems, and local events. They can provide valuable insights into affordable dining options, festivals, and activities off the beaten path.

9. Pack appropriately: Be prepared for different weather conditions by packing appropriate clothing and gear. This ensures you won't have to spend extra money on buying or renting equipment on-site.

10. Stay flexible and open-minded: Be open to spontaneous adventures and last-minute opportunities that may arise during your trip. Stay flexible with your plans, as sometimes the most memorable experiences are unplanned and unexpected.

Remember, exploring the Pyrenees on a budget doesn't mean sacrificing the beauty and adventure of this incredible destination. With careful planning, resourcefulness, and an adventurous spirit, you can have an unforgettable journey without breaking the bank.

Common Tourist Complaints and Solution

Language Barrier

Complaint: Many tourists find it challenging to communicate due to language barriers, especially if they don't speak French or Spanish fluently.

Solution:

a) Learn some basic phrases in French and Spanish before your trip to help you navigate common interactions.

b) Carry a pocket dictionary or language translation app to assist in communication.

c) Seek out tourist information centres where staff members often speak English and can help with translations and recommendations.

Lack of Information and Direction

Complaint: Tourists may struggle to find detailed information or directions for attractions, hiking trails, or public transportation.

Solution:

a) Conduct thorough research in advance and make use of reliable guidebooks, online resources, and official tourism websites to gather relevant information.

b) Seek assistance from tourist information centres or local experts who can provide up-to-date information and maps.

c) Ask for recommendations and directions from locals or fellow travellers who have visited the area before.

Limited Accessibility

Complaint: Some visitors may find that certain attractions or hiking trails in the Pyrenees are not easily accessible or lack proper infrastructure for individuals with mobility challenges.

Solution:

a) Prioritise attractions and trails that are accessible or have alternative routes suitable for different mobility levels.

b) Contact local tourism offices or park authorities in advance to inquire about accessibility options and facilities available.

c) Consider hiring local guides who can provide support and knowledge about accessible routes and activities.

Weather Conditions

Complaint: Unpredictable weather conditions, such as sudden rain or fog, can disrupt outdoor activities and limit visibility, leading to disappointment for tourists.

Solution:

a) Check weather forecasts before heading out and plan accordingly. Be prepared with appropriate clothing and gear for varying weather conditions.

b) Have alternative indoor activities or attractions in mind as backup plans in case of inclement weather.

c) Remain flexible and open to adjusting your itinerary based on the weather conditions to make the most of your trip.

Crowded Tourist Hotspots

Complaint: During peak tourist seasons, popular attractions and hiking trails can become overcrowded, leading to a less enjoyable experience for some visitors.

Solution:

a) Consider visiting during the shoulder seasons when there are fewer crowds.

b) Opt for lesser-known or off-the-beaten-path attractions and hiking trails that offer equally stunning experiences.

c) Plan your visit to popular sites during off-peak hours, such as early mornings or late afternoons, to avoid the busiest times.

Lack of Local Cultural Understanding

Complaint: Tourists may feel disconnected from the local culture and traditions, leading to a sense of missed opportunities for authentic experiences.

Solution:

a) Engage with locals, participate in cultural events, and explore local markets to immerse yourself in the local culture.

b) Respect local customs, traditions, and etiquette by researching and understanding the cultural norms of the region.

c) Seek out authentic local experiences, such as staying in family-run accommodations or joining guided tours led by locals, to gain insights into the local way of life.

By addressing these common complaints with practical solutions, tourists visiting the Pyrenees can enhance their overall experience and ensure a more enjoyable and fulfilling trip to this beautiful mountain range.

CONCLUSION

Your Pyrenean Adventure Awaits!

Embracing the magic and beauty of the Pyrenees has the power to create unforgettable memories and experiences that will stay with you for a lifetime. As you conclude this Pyrenees travel guide, it's time to reflect on the wonders that await you in this breathtaking mountain range.

The Pyrenees offer a diverse range of natural landscapes, from majestic peaks and lush valleys to cascading waterfalls and picturesque villages. Whether you're an outdoor enthusiast seeking thrilling adventures or a culture aficionado looking to immerse yourself in local traditions, the Pyrenees have something for everyone.

From hiking through dramatic canyons and conquering challenging rock faces to biking along scenic trails and indulging in soothing thermal baths, the Pyrenees provide endless opportunities to connect with nature, challenge yourself, and rejuvenate your spirit.

The region's rich history and cultural heritage add an extra layer of charm to your Pyrenean adventure. Explore mediaeval towns, visit ancient monasteries, and savour delicious regional cuisine that showcases the unique flavours of the Pyrenees.

As you plan your dream trip to the Pyrenees, consider the itineraries and suggestions outlined in this guide, but also allow room for serendipity and discovery. The Pyrenees have a way of surprising and delighting travellers with hidden gems and unexpected encounters.

So, start envisioning the breathtaking vistas, the exhilarating outdoor pursuits, and the warm hospitality that await you in the Pyrenees. Begin gathering your gear, researching local customs, and booking accommodations, because your Pyrenean adventure is beckoning.

Whether you're seeking the thrill of outdoor adventures, the tranquillity of nature, or the rich cultural tapestry of the region, the Pyrenees will provide an experience that exceeds your expectations.

So, lace up your hiking boots, secure your climbing harness, and open your heart to the wonders of the Pyrenees. Your journey starts now—embrace the magic and beauty of the Pyrenees and create memories that will last a lifetime.

Start planning your dream trip to the Pyrenees today, and get ready to embark on an extraordinary adventure that will leave you with unforgettable stories and experiences to cherish forever.

Planning to visit other destinations with beautiful mountains, mirror lakes and landscapes? Then check out Alec James, Dolomites.

Que tengas un viaje seguro e increíble, ¡saludos!

avoir un voyage sûr et impressionnant, acclamations!

Date	Itinerary

Made in the USA
Middletown, DE
24 July 2024

57957805R00106